SO-AVG-056

Testimonials

"Shirley Tan is one of the smartest marketers I know. She has this incredible desire to learn and become an expert at whatever she touches. Every time we speak, I learn something from her and her passion for our industry is infectious. If you are in Ecom Hell now, Shirley will show you the way out."

—Joe Tantillo, Greekgear.com

"Shirley Tan is one of the real life e-commerce pioneers who actually managed to build a successful online business and sell it. That experience, coupled with years of work as an e-commerce consultant helping other companies thrive has given her a unique and valuable perspective on the ins and outs of the e-commerce world. If you've ever thought about moving into the e-commerce space, make sure to read this book and give yourself a reality check before you get going."

—Jennifer Evans Cario, Author of
Pinterest Marketing: An Hour a Day

"Shirley possesses unparalleled knowledge of the e-commerce industry on both the micro and macro levels, and she has the unique ability to translate that knowledge into easily consumable pieces of information. I highly recommend this book for beginners and experienced store owners alike!"

—Ezra Firestone, Co-Founder /
Head of Digital Marketing @BOOM! by Cindy Joseph

"Shirley Tan is a pioneering online merchant, having launched her retail bridal site before most us knew what ecommerce was. I have benefited from Shirley's knowledge and experience over the years. And now others will, too, when they read this book. For anyone contemplating a new ecommerce venture, there's no better guide than Shirley."

—Kerry Murdock, Publisher, Practical eCommerce

"Shirley is an incredible entrepreneur that experienced hands on every aspect it takes to make an ecommerce business successful. Regardless of the stage of your ecommerce business, Shirley provides excellent foresight into how to make it to the next level."

—Jennifer Fallon, CEO, The Aspen Brands Company,
KateAspen.com & BabyAspen.com

"We've been a vendor of Shirley's previous business for over 12+ years. Not only have we seen her grow her retail business but impressively watch her catapult her online website beyond the level of any small business we supplied. She understands merchandising, operations and online marketing. We highly recommend for any new start-up to read this book and understand the inner workings of the ecommerce space."

—Serop Beylerian, Co-Founder, Bey-Berk.com

"Shirley Tan is the real deal. As an inquisitive entrepreneur, she always asks all the right questions, and now she is sharing all the right answers for creating a successful ecommerce business. Her book is detailed, insightful, and comprehensive, and will become a must-have for all E-com business owners. Not only has she done it herself, but she knows how to identify and document the things that helped her become successful.

Sharing this wealth of knowledge is only part of what makes her not only a great author, but a great person as well."

—Todd Malicoat, SEO, Faculty Market Motive.com

"If I would have had a book to follow like this when I was starting out in the ecommerce business, I would have a lot more time for business, instead of putting out so many unexpected fires! Bravo to Shirley for telling it like it is 'in the trenches' of the ecommerce business. This book is the real deal, written from an 'all hands on deck' ecommerce professional that has actually lived it, worked it, breathed it and ate it too at times!"

—Pam Marcharola, BlairCandy.com

"Why learn from your own mistakes? You need an experienced guide who will take you through all facets of e-commerce business success. Don't get burned—follow Shirley Tan instead!"

—Tim Ash, CEO of SiteTuners, Author of *Landing Page Optimization*, Chair of Conversion Conference

"Shirley Tan's book, 'Ecom Hell' provides valuable insights from someone who has successfully run her own online store. It is filled with information that any online retailer must know. Often, books of this nature discuss a single aspect of the ecommerce process, but Shirley goes into depth about topics such as setting up your business, stocking your warehouse, handling returns, customer service, human resources, accounting and other business advice that is lacking in many books on ecommerce. An excellent resource that I will recommend to my client.

--- Greg Jameson, CEO, WebStores Ltd., Author of *Grow Your Online Sales*

"Wow, Shirley, where the heck was this when I started my business in 2005? If only I had a complete checklist when I started my business; it took me years of trial and error at the cost of thousands of dollars' worth of frustrating mistakes to figure out even some of the basic information that is included in this book. I'll recommend it to my staff as well as several business owners that I've mentored over the years!"

—Todd Chism,
President, CEO, PatioShoppers.com
Inc. 5000 Fastest Growing Retailers, 2010–2012,
Entrepreneur Magazine's Top Five Emerging
Entrepreneurs of the Year 2006,
Annual Revenue 2012 =$8,600,000.00

ECOM HELL

How To Make Money In Ecommerce Without Getting Burned

SHIRLEY TAN

Copyright Page

Title: Ecom Hell
Subtitle: How to Make Money in Ecommerce without Getting Burned
Author: Shirley Tan
Published by: Shirley Tan, EcommerceSystems.com (Shirleytan@ecommercesystems.com)

All rights reserved. No part of this book may be reproduced or transmitted in any form or by any means, electronic or mechanical, including photocopying, recording, or by any information storage and retrieval system, without written permission from the author, except for the inclusion of brief quotations in a review.

Copyright © 2013 by Shirley Tan:
First Edition, 2013
Published in USA

ISBN: (International Standard Book Number)

ISBN: 0615786871

ISBN 13: 9780615786872

Library of Congress Control Number: 2013935819
ECOM HELL,
San Francisco, CA

Dedication

To all ecommerce entrepreneurs who dare to live their dream and follow their heart for business ownership, may this book guide and inspire you in your new adventure.

To my father, who showed me my entrepreneurial spirit, and to my mother, who taught me my work ethic. To my husband Jeff, I'm the luckiest girl in the world, thank you.

Disclaimer

This book is designed to provide information on general business only. This information is provided and sold with the knowledge that the publisher and author do not offer any legal or other professional advice. In the case of a need for any such expertise, consult with the appropriate professional. This book does not contain all information available on the subject. This book has not been created to be specific to any individual's or organization's situation or needs. Every effort has been made to make this book as accurate as possible. However, there may be typographical and/or content errors. Therefore, this book should serve only as a general guide and not as the ultimate source of subject information. This book contains information that might be dated and is intended only to educate and entertain. The author and publisher shall have no liability or responsibility to any person or entity regarding any loss or damage incurred, or alleged to have incurred, directly or indirectly, by the information contained in this book. You hereby agree to be bound by this disclaimer or you may return this book within the guarantee time period for a full refund.

Table of Contents

SECTION I. WHAT TO CONSIDER BEFORE STARTING AN ECOMMERCE BUSINESS

SECTION III. THE BUSINESS OF ECOMMERCE

Acknowledgments

No one writes a book alone. To the following people, I am indebted for their love, friendship, and support. I would like to thank my husband, Jeff, and my kids, Jon, Aly, and Ethan, for their patience while I spent time on the book and away from them.

I would like to thank my cousins, Macy and Lucy, for loving me like a sister.

I want to thank all my clients over the years who have allowed me to learn from them as much as they have learned from me.

I also want to thank all my mentors who taught me patiently over the years while I learned the ropes.

I am also grateful to:

Bryan Eisenberg, for always answering my pestering questions;

Tim Ash, for encouraging me to write this book in the first place;

Suzie Won, who helped me organize all my crazy notes and thoughts back in the day;

Jessica Bowman, for being my brainstorming partner;

Michael E.Gerber, for awakening the consultant in me;

Michael Gelblicht, for proofreading the book on his own time;

Perry Belcher, who inspired the title;

And finally, the fortune teller who said I would be an author someday—you were right, and I was wrong.

About the Author

Shirley started working at 16 in her family retail hardware store. She then moved to San Francisco, finished college while opening her own retail/wholesale business. She started a mail order catalog business and eventually took that exclusively online. She sold her ecommerce business in 2009 and has been consulting since 2012.

Shirley Tan works as an ecommerce strategist for ecommerce businesses. Growing businesses is her passion. She loves helping entrepreneurs' run and grow their businesses and most of all, helping them be profitable.

"I'm typically brought in when a business is not performing to its full potential," Shirley states.

She works with business owners to evaluate their business strategy and help them creates workflow processes and build a company knowledge base. She does frequently work with family owned business. She also helps develop marketing strategies and designates key performance indicators for tracking and improvement.

Get in touch with Shirley in the following ways:

- Blog: ecommercesystems.com.
- Twitter: @shirleytan
- Facebook: Facebook.com/ecommercesystems
- LinkedIn: linkedin.com/in/shirleytan
- Email: shirleytan@ecommercesystems.com

Foreword

Global e-commerce, including travel and auto purchases as well as online retail sales, will reach an estimated $1.4 trillion in 2015, according Cisco Systems Inc.'s Economics & Research Practice. You've probably been dreaming about how you capture your share of this incredible growth. A retail transformation unlike any other in the history of trade is unfolding in front of our very own eyes.

You likely have some premise of how easy selling is online or how you can become wealthy while working in your underwear from home. While e-commerce eliminates many of the challenges a traditional brick and mortar retail shop possesses, it certainly is not as simple as it looks. If you are looking to create the type of experience that has your customers delighted to shop with you, sharing their great experiences with friends and returning to buy from you again, all while making a healthy profit you better pay attention to the lessons Shirley Tan shares with you in Ecom Hell.

I've known Shirley for nearly 8 years, when she owned her own "little" ecommerce shop, which she turned into a very attractive acquisition for a NASDAQ traded publishing conglomerate. She started as 2 person retailer and exploded to over 30 full time employees not counting outside contractors. She shares not only her ecommerce knowledge accumulated over the span of 20+ years but also shares her success and failures so that you can hopefully avoid some of the ecommerce hell she went through.

- **Bryan Eisenberg**, New York Times Best Selling Author, Keynote Speaker

Introduction

It's what you don't know that hurts you—or *sends you to Ecom Hell*. So in order to help you avoid ending up in Ecom Hell muttering, "I didn't know about that," I have filled this book with a "road map" of directions and road signs—operational and growth tips, checklists, and best practices for your ecommerce venture.

Because I have been down the road to Ecom Hell, I know that these lists and tips are the best directions for keeping you from making a wrong turn.

I recommend that you read through everything first to get a general idea of what running an ecommerce business involves. Then, as you develop your company, you can return to specific chapters as needed. I wrote the book with certain assumptions that my audience would have prior business experience not necessarily owning their own business but worked in other businesses. This book is meant to be a guide and to give entrepreneurs wanting to get into ecommerce a good look on what is involve in starting and growing an ecommerce business. The book is not intended to be in-depth coverage for each type of marketing or search engine optimization, or even general management. There are many wonderful and informative books online for you to study and become an expert in specific areas. The goal of this book is to ensure you have more than enough tools to get you started and that you're not getting into this new venture unarmed.

Consider the tips, homework, checklist as reference aids pointing you in the right direction. You can then use what you learned here to do further research on any of the topics covered when the time is right for you. (For more in-depth learning on any of the topics covered, check out the resources section, where I provide information to additional material by other experts).

About The Title

I believe business success is a combination of strategic planning and excellent execution, helped often by a heavy dose of optimism. I understand the value of optimism as it carries many an entrepreneur through a rough day or two. However, I also believe is anticipating worst case scenarios to avoid them at all costs. This is the impetus behind Ecom Hell: I'll help you face the pitfalls that can be part of ecommerce business building; and give you the best practices to use to navigate your way around these potentially hellish situations. Ecom Hell is going to help you build your own ecom heaven.

Section I.

What to Consider before Starting an Ecommerce Business

Chapter 1.

To Hell and Back: Where I Came from

I did not start out in hell or with any idea that I would end up there. I stumbled upon retail in the late 1980s, when I set up a retail gift shop to get myself through college. After graduating from college with a degree in business, I left my retail store with a friend and business partner while I went home to help my parents with the family business. My logic at the time was that my family's was a "real" business, whereas mine was just a hobby making a little money on the side. My goal was to use my newly learned business skills to help my family become more successful.

As anyone who's ever worked in a family business can attest, trying to coach your parents on how to run their business can send you spinning into *hell*. In the end, I felt that I'd rather jump off a bridge than continue to bang my head against that brick wall. Needless to say, working in the family biz didn't work out for me; I returned to my "part-time" business with more conviction than ever that I would make things work "for real" this time.

I plodded along for some time with my brick-and-mortar business, trying to grow the company within the four walls of the retail/wholesale space. The problem with the storefront business model, however, is that on any given day, if nobody walks into the store, there are no sales or income.

Despite the slow days, we plodded on and survived several recessions, yet I was very dissatisfied; I knew I had to find a way to get more sales and reach customers nationwide.

In addition to the retail gift shop, my business partner and I developed a wedding accessories catalog that targeted wedding consultants and brides. We were generating some sales through a mail-order catalog and had a few consultants selling our products for a commission. But the mail-order catalog business model is tough, and I got tired of the tedious process of sorting bulk mail.

In 1996, on the suggestion of a friend, we registered our company name online as a .com URL at Network Solutions. We eventually got our store up online, and AmericanBridal.com was born. However, at that time, the online business still took a backseat to our main brick-and-mortar retail business.

In those days, the Internet was going through a transformation. Consumers were beginning to see higher connection speeds than 56K dial-up modems. Bandwidth to the home steadily increased, thanks to emerging broadband cable and DSL Internet services, and this enabled access to more robust online content, such as images and graphics. Consequently, people started to enjoy shopping online. Then, in late 2001, Amazon.com reported turning a profit for the first time after six years in business! The online retail market was young and ripe with opportunity.

A Trip to Hell in One Day

By 2004, I had been in retail for about eighteen years and was tired of the storefront business. So I sold the brick-and-mortar portion to my partner but kept the online part of the business. Then, the very month I took over AmericanBridal.com on my own, the site was gone from Google. This happened on April Fools' Day (*I kid you not*), but it wasn't a joke and not at all funny. In fact, it was *hell*. Instantly, traffic ceased and there were almost no visitors or income.

This trip to hell led me to pour every part of my being into learning how to get featured back on Google. I devoted myself to learning search engine marketing and search engine optimization. A key lesson I learned during this baptism-by-fire period was the importance of search engines in marketing my ecommerce site. This was also a huge revelation about online business in general.

Even though my business had begun as brick-and-mortar and had then evolved to add ecommerce, it didn't take me long to realize that I would have to treat the ecommerce side as a new business and build it from scratch.

I decided to work backward; before building an entire business infrastructure with operations, finance, and customer service, I first had to research the market and determine demand for products online. Thanks to the free- or low-cost keyword and analytics services available, I could do keyword research (what people are searching for online) to determine what I would sell online, even before setting up a business, buying a domain name, hiring a web developer, and so on.

After the Google debacle, I also took time to find the right consultants and information to help build my business from scratch. Then, by putting everything I learned into practice, I was able to climb out of hell slowly and recovered from being absent on Google. From there, my employees and I focused on providing better merchandising, better images, and better product descriptions then our online business took off.

The success I then experienced was so phenomenal that from 2004 to 2008, my little company moved four times and grew from a staff of just five people to thirty employees, as we struggled to stay on top of orders.

During this journey, I learned quite a few lessons—some the hard way and others simply by being in the right place at the right time. I got to know myself a lot better and discovered my true capacity as an entrepreneur. I learned that the more I was challenged, the more I could achieve. I also learned that selling to a niche market, rather than trying to be all things to all people, is a much more lucrative endeavor for cash-sensitive entrepreneurs.

In 2009, I sold my ecommerce business, which consisted of seven different websites, to a NASDAQ-listed corporation. I will give you more details later about why I wanted to sell my growing business and what it took to sell the company for what I thought it was worth.

Since 2012, I have worked as a consultant, using the lessons I learned on my own journey to help other aspiring entrepreneurs, just like you, establish their own successful ecommerce sites. Every small business must work within what is often a strapped budget and with low capital. I have learned, and proven, that to get the most bang for your investment buck, targeting a niche market results in less competitive keywords, more conversions, and a much better opportunity to emerge as a market leader. If in some small way, this book helps contribute to your own ecommerce success (without all the hell I experienced along the way), that will be immensely gratifying to me.

Chapter 2.

If You Can't Stand the Heat…Stay out of Hell: The Most Important People in Your Business

Your company's most valuable asset is how it is known to its customers.

—Brian Tracy

When my associates or clients are sizing up an ecommerce business, whether starting one or buying an existing operation, I ask them why they are choosing ecommerce. Frequently, I have heard a response similar to either "Because I am tired of dealing with customers," or "So I will not have to deal with people face to face."

You need to know that this is a big misconception. The image conjured up by many prospective ecommerce entrepreneurs is that they will be able to work at home and hide behind a computer with little or no contact and no need to "deal with" customers. An ecommerce business is all about customers, and every one of them is your boss.

Let's face it; customers are not always right, *but* customers will always be customers. We all know that dealing with the various comments and criticisms of consumers is not the most pleasant aspect of owning a business. And customers seem to hold all the power over the success of your business. Yet, it is within your power to turn your customers into either raving fans or critical detractors.

To succeed in creating, maintaining, and increasing your fan base, you must do everything to cater to their demands before satisfying your own. Therefore, unless you are willing to accommodate an infinite number of needs and bear an infinite number of blows, do not expect your business to stay out of hell.

Hot Tip: Do not start an ecommerce business if you hate dealing with customers.

Think of all the successful websites around today—Amazon, Facebook, Yelp, YouTube, and Zappos, to name just a few. All of these sites cater to the user, and each site's value proposition lies in the fact that the site is all about the visitor. For example, Amazon sells just about anything you would want to buy. Amazon's investor relations home page states its value proposition as: *"We seek to be Earth's most customer-centric company for three primary customer sets: consumer customers, seller customers, and developer customers."*

Facebook and YouTube let you post as much information about yourself as you want to share, including favorites (movies, music, food, etc), photos, status updates, and videos.

Zappos arose from the founder's frustrating experience in trying to find the right pair of shoes at a mall. The company is now legendary for excellent customer service and customer-centric policies.

Yelp relies on customers' restaurant reviews for most content.

See…Business is all about them, the customers. This simple yet elegant formula hearkens back to old-fashioned customer-centric values. Get the picture?

If you do share the values of these successful customer-centric websites, you are a prime candidate to set up shop and get your share of online sales, which, according to Forrester,[1] are expected to top $229 billion by the end of 2013 in the United States alone.

With the popularity of social media, ecommerce is evolving as the web continues to provide forums for consumer discussions and product reviews, all of which help to fuel a brand's momentum. Social-media marketing, which we will discuss in more detail later, is another great way to increase awareness of your brand through online networks, such as Facebook, Twitter, and so forth.

You do need a professional-looking site that is user-friendly, converts well, and loads quickly. You also need a well-oiled marketing strategy. But all benefits from that are lost if your site does not focus on providing a solution your customer is seeking. If your site sells pretty things that your customers do not want to buy or if you fail to ship your orders in a timely manner, you will visit hell.

A question I have been asked is: "But I already have a retail store. Is an ecommerce business right for me?"

My simple answer is *yes*! If you already have a retail store, that is all the more reason to create an online ecommerce presence. Not only will ecommerce drive additional revenue when your physical stores are closed; it will also direct traffic back to your brick-and-mortar storefront.

As a smaller business, you can succeed more easily by focusing on niche categories; that is the area where big-box stores cannot compete and where the most flexible company wins. In general, smaller companies are nimbler, move faster, and are more flexible than larger corporations. Small businesses can adapt more quickly, spot growing trends, and jump on opportunities before the market gets saturated.

Hot Tip: You do not have to be first; you just have to be better.

Today's customers are looking for value, savings, and reliability; they want all the things they can get from a brick-and-mortar store, plus more. With an online presence, you can do all this faster. They want to know they can trust you to ship their orders in a timely fashion. Focus on

---

1 www.bizreport.com/2010/11/reports-q3-eCommerce-growth-steady-q4-forecast-strong.html.

providing the most value for their money, and your online store will be successful.

PS: Value is what the customer perceives it to be, not what you think it is. Provide them a solution they want, and you're golden.

Chapter 3.

The Road to Hell Is Paved: Making a Plan

If you think education is expensive, try ignorance.

—Harvey Mackay

Maybe you have heard the saying, "The road to hell is paved with good intentions." Ask any of the 90 percent of business owners who fail in the first three years of their business and I am sure they will tell you they thought at the time that everything they were doing was according to a plan. While they had the passion and motivation, or "good intentions," they lacked the necessary knowledge and tools to stay out of hell.

Budgeting: Planning Your Initial Investment

You might be surprised at how many entrepreneurs fail to put a budget on paper. They figure that they have everything in their head and since a budget is a projection anyway, why bother? But you should never start an ecommerce business if you refuse to create an initial budget and sales/ expense projections.

Hot Tip: Don't start an ecommerce business unless you're willing to write a business plan and create an initial financial projection.

Even if you do not know the exact numbers, you can at least figure out what you will need to start and maintain your business. This will help prevent you from burning through your cash and needing more capital infusion either through a loan or angel money from family and friends. A business plan is a road map to help you stay focused on your business goals. It is your guide for taking action on your strategies.

If you lack a written budget, you have no business borrowing from family and friends. There! I have said it. A budget will help you figure out whether your business goals are achievable. A budget will also help you decide which direction you should head: Do you sell to the masses at low margins? Or do you sell fewer widgets at higher margins but to a smaller customer base? These are the kind of questions that get answered when you have a business plan.

How Much Money You Need to Get Started and Avoid Hell

To start your ebusiness, you need capital. The amount will vary depending on whether you are starting from the ground up or you are moving an existing business online. When setting up your business, be frugal no matter how much capital you might have. Many expenses will pop up down the road, so do not blow your entire budget on that fancy new office furniture just yet. Remember, your goal is to build a strong, lasting organization; achieving success on a shoestring budget is pretty rare these days.

Since we are on the topic of finances, let me say up front that I will not be shy about giving advice on frugality, but when I tell you not to compromise on quality and reliability to save money, that comes from the perspective of a business owner who has experienced the pain of making the wrong decision. Save yourself the headaches and heed my advice in such areas. Throughout this book, I will remind you now and again to keep a tight watch on your expenses because what really matters is not how much you make or sell, but how much you keep, that is, your net profit.

Even if you are setting up an online store, you still need an office and possibly even storage space. Check Craigslist for free or low-cost preowned office furniture. Bring in your extra coffeemaker, microwave oven, and toaster from home. Ask friends whether they are planning to get rid of any furniture, fax machines, printers, or other office supplies and offer to haul them away. Barter where you can for services and goods. For larger contracts, however, such as a lease, consult an attorney.

If you plan to drop ship your products, hold inventory, or do a little bit of both, you will have to find some storage space. This could be in your garage or a proper storage or warehouse space. Again, consult an attorney for any lease contracts. If you have not already sourced inventory, line up a few vendors and make sure you understand their terms of service.

Setting up your business also includes establishing your online presence. Invest wisely in website design and development, because that's your storefront where you will merchandise your products for sale. Behind the scenes of your web store is the back end, which includes order-management software, an accounting system, fulfillment, shipping, and customer service.

Once your online store is built, with back end and front end operating cohesively, you will need to promote your business. Internet marketing, specifically, pay-per-click (PPC), email marketing, social media and search engine optimization (SEO), will be front and center to promoting your new online business.

Managing Your Time

In running a business, a common mistake is to address time management issues somewhere in the middle of a project or afterward in a postmortem state, when costly mistakes have been made and lessons learned. To help you avoid those expensive mistakes, I'm going to cover the topic here early so I can help you have a better experience from the start.

Eight Steps to Efficient Time Management

1. Identify clear goals and future milestones that you want your business to achieve.
2. Create a strategy to achieve those goals. Break it down into smaller groups, departments, or categories.
3. Identify tactical strategies, steps, or tasks that require completion to achieve your goals.
4. Sort and prioritize your tactical strategies.
5. Block out time and set deadlines for completing each task.
6. Whenever possible, delegate tasks. Ensure that instructions and goals are clear.
7. Don't take on too many open tasks at once. This will only lead to confusion and lots of incomplete tasks. Multi-tasking is the enemy of productivity.
8. Keep a daily work diary. Write down every task that you handle. At the end of each week, assign a value to each task indicating which tasks can be delegated or outsourced. When making this type of decision, think about what your time is worth. For example, is your time better spent focusing on marketing or filing paperwork?

Time Management Tips

- Keep your working space organized.
- File papers promptly, or set a time to file papers all at once. Don't let that paperwork pile up. Get into the filing habit now, while your company is still small. This will also set a good example for your employees to follow.
- Return emails and calls promptly, ideally within twenty-four hours. Set a time to do this but not first thing in the morning. I found that when I would answer calls first thing, I would get distracted by what other people wanted or needed me to do and my to-do list would get pushed back or put off. The best time to answer the phone or reply to emails is after you got your priority items done or started as sometimes you're also waiting on others input.

- Don't be a busybody. Instead, focus on accomplishing things. In other words, focus on productivity.

Getting Started Checklist

☐ Research your business/industry, and determine what you're going to sell.

☐ Capital—How much money do you have/need to invest in the business?

    ☐ For inventory?

    ☐ For employees?

    ☐ For marketing your new business?

☐ Know your burn rate. How fast are you spending money versus what is coming in?

☐ Register for a business license and legal entity.

☐ Online storefront platform—Research and find the best one you can afford. (See chapter 8 for features and functionality requirements)

Your Homework

1. Decide whether you are going to buy an existing business or start one from scratch. If the former, go to a website that sells businesses to see what kinds are for sale and how much they cost.
2. Get your finances in order, and decide how much money you are going to invest in this new business.

As much as I hate to be negative at this stage when you're supposed to be excited about your business prospects, now is a good time to review the sobering reasons that many ecommerce businesses fail. (Keep this list in an obvious place to help you stay focused. You will face many difficult business decisions along the way, but you'll at least know to avoid the following scenarios.)

Top Ten Reasons Ecommerce Businesses End Up in Hell

1. Inadequate research on product profitability and margins—too much emphasis on sales and not enough on profitability
2. Lack of specialization—trying to appeal to too broad an audience
3. Inappropriate website design or layout that results in bad user experience and poor conversion
4. Lack of originality or unique and compelling content (weak unique selling proposition)—Me too website
5. Inflexible ecommerce platform
6. Poor customer service
7. Inferior supply chain or inventory management
8. Poor execution
9. Not enough capital
10. Underestimating the competition

Chapter 4.

Do Not Buy a Ticket to Hell: Buying a Business Versus Building One

A large number of businesses close their doors before their first anniversary, and estimates are that almost 90 percent fail in the first three years. So buying an existing business with things in place, such as a positive cash flow, can be a huge advantage—but not just any business.

Make sure the business you are considering is not already in hell or headed there. Unless you are extremely savvy and experienced, do not buy a business in hell thinking you can resuscitate it or one headed to hell thinking you can change the direction.

If you have the cash or financing, you can buy an existing ecommerce business. Either way, be sure to conduct due diligence. When looking at an existing business, verify revenue against bank deposits, study analytics and tax returns, research keywords, talk to vendors, and verify margins and study trends, just as you would when starting from scratch. I also recommend that you shadow the company that you are planning to acquire. This will give you insights on how well things are being run, what kind of problems exist, and whether those problems are easy to fix. Think about whether you will need more capital to address any ongoing issues. Review the organization's business process and training material.

Many businesses for sale are advertised as "turnkey," but I caution you to evaluate the accuracy of this claim carefully. To me, turnkey translates to sales that are deposited from the old owner's bank account into your bank account after the sale of the business has been completed. Turnkey means that the business keeps running as usual, just under new ownership. Usually, all the employees stay to run the business just as before, but now you are the owner.

Do not consider buying an online business solely because the website has good search rankings. This means the website shows up high on the first page for search results for specific keywords. Ask for historical ranking reports to ensure that you know and understand how the website ranked over time. Don't forget to review inventory value, inventory turnover, and stale/dated inventory as well.

Check the company's unique value proposition (the why-people-should-buy-from-you factor). Ask whether you can observe the business for a few days to see if what they do is a good fit for you.

Is the seller financing part of the sale? If so, be extra sure to consult a business broker or an attorney with experience in this type of transaction.

The advantage of buying an existing ecommerce business is that you will have a track record of a proven business concept and historical data on what has worked and what has not, not to mention existing revenue. The disadvantage is that there might be some legacy systems or inherent issues that were not disclosed. Also keep in mind that if you buy a business and then relocate, you might lose the existing knowledge base of the employees who leave.

Tips on Buying an Existing Ecommerce Business

- Know, understand, and document all company debt and assets.
- Write to suppliers to verify balances owed to them.
- Contact the current landlord on the seller's lease and ask questions:
  - Will the landlord allow you to take over?

- Will the landlord raise the rent?
- Will the landlord let you off the lease?
- If you plan to move the business, determine whether existing employees will relocate with you.
- Uncover any liens that might be against the existing business.
- Find out whether there are any prior or current lawsuits or legal claims against the business.
- Ask whether the seller will finance part of the sale.
- Are you requiring an earn-out—certain revenue or goals to be achieved to get additional "x" (usually additional premium payment)?
- List all assets that you are acquiring to avoid any confusion or misunderstanding.
- Verify all past revenue claims. Review and compare analytics data on revenue against financial statements. Get the past three years' tax returns of the business and personal returns of the owners.
- Verify and audit all bank statements related to the business (deposits, checks written out, and so on).
- Audit the top two hundred products for margin markup against the selling price or top 20% of the inventory that comprise of 80% of the company's revenue.
- Audit the inventory's historical value. Don't agree to pay for obsolete or stale inventory—that is, anything more than one year old. If something didn't sell for an entire year, it's not likely to start selling now.
- Do a physical count of the inventory that you will be acquiring.
- Hire your own attorney to review or write out the purchase contracts.
- Hire a search engine optimization (SEO) expert to audit the website to ensure that it has a clean history.
- Review social network comments about the existing business to evaluate the customers' perception of it.
- Research any potential competitors who can easily come into the market and steal your lunch.
- Find out what kinds of patents and trademarks the business owns.
- Ask about other distribution points that might require additional resources, manpower, and energy. Does the business import goods

and sell wholesale as well as online? Keep in mind that the wholesale business is very different from retail and online business.

- Find out who the business's strategic partners are. What ongoing and current contracts are in place to support this alliance?
- Ask about any promises and commitments that have been made to current employees. Do you need to honor these commitments?
- Consider the barrier to entry. How easy would it be for someone to copy this business model?
- Determine if there is any special knowledge or skill set that the current owner has that you do not have. Can you learn it, or will you need to hire additional help?
- Determine the unique value proposition. Why is this business special? Why do customers keep coming back time and again?
- Look at production issues. If the business manufactures a product or even tweaks it a bit (personalization is a great way to add value), review the production schedule, reports, equipment condition, equipment warranty, employee work shifts, and capacity level.
- Interview a few key suppliers. What is the company's reputation among its vendors?
- Don't get into a bidding war for a business if you can avoid it.
- Ask for a list of all software and technology used to include license number, user name and passwords.

From a buyers prospective, it's great if you can require an earn-out provision, but from a seller's prospective its not a good requirement to agree to. More on this in Chapter 24 on Selling your business.

A Word about Partners

If you are going into a partnership with a friend or a family member or even buying into an existing business as a partner, think twice and then think again.

I had a successful business partnership for eighteen years; it worked out for us because we brought different skill sets to the business. Just like with most new marriages, individuals go into partnership with lots of hope and good intentions, and just like most marriages, businesses have challenges. When things are bad, it can get *really* bad.

If you decide to have a partner, choose someone who will offset your weaknesses and share your values. What assets or skill sets (money, expertise, etc) do each of you bring to the business? Remember, things will go much easier when you can focus on the external competition and not on internal bickering between you and your partner.

If you are considering partnering with a family member, you might be in for one *hell* of a time—and not in a good way.

Whether you are going into business with a friend, family member, or complete stranger, make sure you have a very clear, written expectation agreement. Also include a breakup clause or a partnership dissolution clause. Agree ahead of time on how the partnership will dissolve if required. For example, you buy out your partner at such-and-such a price or vice versa, or the partnership gets sold according to a binding mediation order.

Discussing this at the start, while you are both eager and cooperative, is much better, as that enables you to reach a fairer arrangement. If you cannot come to a fair arrangement, then avoid moving forward with the partnership; you will end up in *hell* for sure.

Hot Tip: Trust is the most important factor you must have in a partnership. If you and your partner/family member can have these tough conversations from the start, the chances of having a successful partnership are higher.

Chapter 5.

Market Research and Business Concepts to Stay out of Hell

You will languish in Ecom Hell if: *you are not willing to do the research needed.*

In addition to being able to avoid facing the customer, other misconceptions about ecommerce businesses are that they do not require as much research as a "regular" business and that they run themselves. The fact is an ecommerce business requires just as much research as other business models and they do not "run themselves." Business is all about working hard up front and then reaping the rewards of what you have sown. If you do not have the dedication and the patience to work first and play later, you will likely end up in Ecom Hell.

As you would for any project, be prepared to do your research before beginning your business. This includes researching product sourcing, vendors, software solutions, keywords, and competitors, as well as knowing as much as you possibly can about each topic. Knowledge is power, and the goal is to "crush it". The bottom line: The more prepared you are, the more likely you are to avoid *hell* and achieve success.

Now that you have decided that ecommerce is right for you, what will you sell? Many ecommerce stores are started out of necessity, usually by someone who could not find a particular item, so he or she decided to open an ecommerce store to fill that very same demand. Could this be you? Think about your passions. Do you collect something that others are also shopping for? Starting with an area you are already knowledgeable about is a safer bet.

Do you have something unique (unique selling proposition) to offer or sell, or can you serve a particular market better than the competition can? One factor that contributes to online business success is your ability to be a thought leader or go-to person in the industry. Do you have any hobbies within a certain niche? Do you have a source for these products?

Niche Markets

While this might seem counterintuitive, setting up an ecommerce store to cater to a niche market is more likely to position your business for success than trying to be too broad. Many large stores, like Amazon and Target, have the massive buying power, infrastructure, and marketing budget to outsell their competition. But if you focus on serving a niche, you are marketing your goods to highly targeted customers. Finding a niche market will help your business stand out from the crowd. Focus on expanding a niche category for which big brands only carry a few selections.

Research will be needed to uncover a niche market with a demand that is not being adequately met. Get insights from discussion boards and forums about business opportunities. If consumers are voicing their frustration about an unfulfilled need, act quickly to find a way to offer your solution. Read *Blue Ocean Strategy* by W. Chan Kim and Renée Mauborgne, a book about company positioning and competition. This book basically asks whether you want to compete in a sea of red, in which there is a lot of competition, or you are going to position your company in the blue ocean, where there is either very little competition or you own the space completely.

The most obvious place to look when choosing a niche is within your own interests. Are you into dogs? Then consider a business that has something to do with pet supplies. Intimate knowledge about a particular niche service can help define your unique selling proposition. Being passionate about the product or service can only help your business, because you will have a unique insight into both the customer base and the products you offer.

In addition, pick a niche that has the potential for repeat business, which is vital to profitability. Examples of such products include books, clothing, health and beauty products, vitamins, printer cartridges and toner, products that require refills, and so on. Evergreen categories and consumed products are other ideal reorder candidates. Offer a subscription, auto-order, or ship feature for repeat customers for steady sales that you can count on. This is one area that most entrepreneurs overlook, because they are strictly looking at that first sale and not subsequent sales. Evaluate to see if your product category lends itself to multiple units sold. This will bring up your average order value. As an example of this is I had sold bridesmaid gifts, which lends itself to multiple units as the average bridesmaids in a wedding party is around 3-5.

The fashion category can be lots of fun and profitable. You just have to have a good pulse on the latest fashion trends. However, customers are finicky, and this business requires lots of updating. It can be a hit-or-miss proposition. I once had a fashion bag site, and I found staying on top of the latest trends a constant challenge.

Other ways to find out about niche markets is to attend a trade show for the industry in which you are interested. For example, for the gift industry, there is the Americas Mart gift show in Atlanta or the New York International Gift Fair. There are also smaller regional gift shows, such as the San Francisco International Gift Fair. Attending any of these shows will give you a chance to see upcoming products and determine whether you can catch the wave before a product really takes off. Observe which booths are the busiest. Which brands look familiar to you? Have you seen them in a local store or online? I had a friend who started his business during the early days of the "pet rock." Almost thirty years later, he has used that phenomenon as a launch pad to his current business.

Branding is the battle of perception not products. Too many entrepreneurs think that if they can just get to the customer then the customer will realize that they have the better product over the competition. Unfortunately, it doesn't really work that way. Branding is about gaining mindshare, being the default company when consumers think about those products in the category of business that you're in. Your goal with your marketing effort is to have your brand be perceived at the #1 in the category that you're competing in.

If you're getting into a category that is already very crowded, but you're still not deterred, then you have to position your brand as the alternate to whomever is already perceived as #1. You have to be deliberate about contrasting your company to theirs. What makes your company different even though you're selling almost the same thing? This is a a good to know while you're still in the early state of doing your research. One of the things we were able to contrast our services was that we let the customer personalize their gift however they like while the competitors were limiting their customers to what made it easy for them to standardize.

One last tip when looking for a niche market: The more labor-intensive the category, the less competition you will have. The bigger players are not interested in labor-intensive categories like product personalization, so there will be more opportunity for you to carve out a business opportunity for yourself.

Initial Criteria for Vetting a Niche Category's Viability

- Is the average product selling price thirty-five dollars and up?
- Is the potential for reorders high?
- Is the potential to cross-market into another category high (e.g., home-improvement products)?
- Is your product consumable?
- Does your product have an expiration date?
- Is there a wide pricing structure for merchandise so that you can increase the average order value (AOV)?
- Can products be shipped in small packages so that you don't get clobbered on shipping costs? (For example, furniture is a nice

category, but shipping furniture can be very costly and has a high damage rate.)

The key is to try to extend the lifetime value of the customer. If the customer will order only one time from you, you might not go to *hell* or *heaven* for that matter, because you cannot afford a trip.

If the customer orders six or more times, you can amortize the acquisition over the frequency of the customer order, thereby making the cost of acquiring this customer's business less and less over time. The less acquiring a sale costs you, the more money you make.

To brainstorm possible niche markets, make a list under each of the following headings:

- Areas of interest or hobbies
- Areas of knowledge or expertise (for example, *"People always call me to learn about..."*)
- Problems that your business solves for others or needs your business fulfills in the marketplace

Using Keyword Research to Determine a Niche

Search engines use keywords on the site to determine what the site is about and rank them accordingly based on their proprietary algorithms. Moz.com cites over 200 factors that Google may use in its closely guarded proprietary algorithm. You can learn more about search engine optimization online. There are voluminous articles and books on this subject. I will cover the basics to get you started as the main emphasis of this book is about comprehensive ecommerce business and not a deep analysis of a particular area.

A good idea is not enough; you need to test your niche idea. How do you know whether there is a market for your niche product or service? One way is to search for related keywords. The Google AdWords keyword tool can help you identify whether there is a significant number of keyword searches related to your product. Are other businesses satisfying this demand? If so, what keywords are they using?

Keywords are not only useful for determining whether there is a market; they can also help you understand critical factors, such as profitability, reorder potential, and seasonality of your particular market.

Long-tail keywords are highly defined keywords (longer phrases) related to your main keyword that can help further define your niche. Unlike short-tail keywords, which are just a single, general term or two, long-tail keywords are less competitive. For example, typing the short-tail keyword "paper clips" will return two million search results. That's too competitive! However, a search on the keywords "novelty paper clips" returns fewer than two hundred thousand search results. This is still a large number but segmented enough to be your niche. Fewer results from a keyword search mean less competition, giving you a better chance of ranking higher in Google and outperforming your competitors.

The first stage of developing a keyword strategy is brainstorming. At this stage, you are trying to come up with a list of search term contenders.

The next step is to cull the list by focusing on the most frequently used and relevant terms people search to find what you offer.

Main Terms (single keywords and short phrases)

One of the most common mistakes made by those new to keyword search marketing is trying to focus on a single word (like *uniforms*) or phrase (like *gold jewelry*) and then attempting to build a website that will rank well from that word or phrase. Extremely general terms like these are not only very competitive; they are also difficult to rank for on search engines (that is, in terms of providing relevant results to searchers). So don't spend your marketing budget and time trying to target a broad keyword term.

Let's say, hypothetically, that after spending hundreds of hours tweaking and loads of money perfecting and promoting your site, you manage to rank number one for the keyword "uniforms." However, unless you sell every kind of uniform ever made and worn around the world, a majority of the traffic you get will come from those looking for something you do not offer. Thus, they most likely will not become customers.

Even if you don't optimize your site for general keywords, you need to know what they are and how they apply to your site. In the homework that follows, list the five to ten "major" keywords that describe your website. These major search terms, which should be mostly single words (such as *clothing*), with a couple of common phrases (like womens clothes) thrown in, collectively define the themes around which you will organize your site's content. If you leave out any major terms, do not worry; this is an area you can easily add to later.

Google AdWords Keyword Tool

The keywords you choose will be determined by a combination of factors, including the nature of your products. You will not be very successful optimizing a page if the keywords you select are not reflected in the page's content. The beauty of keyword research is that you can find out from search engines like Google which terms or words consumers are searching for to find products. For example, think about the last time you searched for a particular item online. Did you type the generic name (kitchen mixer) or a brand name (KitchenAid)?

Keyword Research Tips

- Optimize a small set of proven keywords and focus on conversion optimization, landing-page testing to improve your conversion rates incrementally. Personally, I can only manage a set of around seven hundred to one thousand keywords, even if I break them up into different smaller campaigns.
- Set up daily and monthly budgets for each keyword research campaign. Don't forget to adjust the budget and move more funds into campaigns that are converting and reduce the budget for those that are not converting as well or at all.
- Create a negative keyword list. For example, *wedding* is a pretty general keyword that would prove too costly to be allowed in your ad campaign if your company only sells wedding favors. This information will be useful when you're ready to do pay-per-click advertising.
- Think about all the variations people could possibly concoct, including misspellings, symbols in place of letters, and so forth.

To summarize, if your website can be found online, your chances of staying out of hell and succeeding will multiply greatly. That's why I walked you through keyword research before going through the traditional market research exercise. What you might have gleaned from doing keyword research is to find out if there is potential in this keyword cateogory to create a business. What you're looking for is to identify with a community of enough people who share common interests and concerns that will potential buy from you.

Keyword List Homework

- List five to ten major keywords that describe your site's products/services.
- Research active communities online, forums and blogs using the keyword lists that you found.
- Research which websites are using these same keywords.

- Expand the smaller subset of similar keywords to better understand how big the marketplace is for the keywords you're investigating.

Set Up a Test Website as an Affiliate

One way to research whether your business idea is viable is to create an affiliate website or to become an affiliate for another website. Once you have a general idea about what products you want to sell, you can set up a test website to try out keywords that are most likely to direct traffic and visitors to your site. Your website does not have to have all the bells and whistles; at this juncture, you are just testing to see if there is demand for the products you want to sell. It might cost you a few hundred dollars to have a test ecommerce store, but that is better than investing tens of thousands or more in a real store just to know if there's a market.

Since this is a test site, you will not need to procure actual products, but you will need to populate the site with some content about the products you wish to sell. For example, if you want to sell cooking products, set up a food blog with recipes that call for the use of specific kitchen gadgets and cookware.

Then, to truly test your concept, set up affiliate accounts with big-box retailers in the same industry (e.g., Williams Sonoma; Bed, Bath and Beyond; Crate and Barrel). Likewise, becoming an affiliate of an existing, well-established ecommerce site, which in some cases might be your competitors, will enable you to "sell" products to see how effective your site is at attracting and converting customers. You can also sign up with affiliate program administrators, such as LinkShare, Commission Junction, or Google Affiliate Network, to name a few.

By the way, you're not losing money here. With an affiliate link, if someone reading your recipe clicks on a product link embedded with your unique affiliate code and makes a purchase, you will get a commission for that sale. Sound good? Well, keep reading because how well you do here can help you decide whether your niche is going to be profitable.

Because traffic for the sake of traffic means very little in the ecommerce world, you will want to test for conversion, or those visitors who become paying customers by making a purchase. You can use pay-per-click (PPC) to test for converting keywords and then measure for margin and calculate return on investment (ROI, or how much the keyword costs versus how much you make from using the word). I will cover PPC in greater detail later.

You're probably wondering why I asked you to go through the affiliate route and keyword research first. I have spoken with so many entrepreneurs who later discovered that the niche market they got into was not profitable. They may have stumbled into an opportunity or just copied another website because they thought it was a good idea. Either way, looking at another website from the outside doesn't give you any insight. Therefore it's much better to do a test pilot to determine if your business model is not only a good idea, but is profitable one as well.

Chapter 6.

How to Be Sure as Hell: Analyzing Yourself and the Competition

You will struggle in Ecom Hell if: *you do not have a tough conversation with yourself about your business.*

Sizing Up the Competition and Yourself

And while the law of competition may be sometimes hard for the individual, it is best for the race, because it ensures the survival of the fittest in every department.

—Andrew Carnegie

Competitive analysis is critical to any business. In the ecommerce world, you have a lot of tools at your disposal for this task. First off, you can immediately become a customer by visiting competitors' websites, making purchases, and even signing up for their email newsletter. If you became an affiliate of a competitor site as part of the test website and keyword research, you're that much closer to understanding the competition.

Install Google Analytics or other analytic tools on your test website to study user behavior and traffic source. These tools make measurement easier than ever before. In fact, this unprecedented access to data means that everyone should be conducting thorough research on competitors. Once you are comfortable with your keyword research, perform a SWOT (strengths, weaknesses, opportunities, and threats) analysis to identify factors that could help your business succeed, as well as those that could send you to hell if you ignore them.

Performing a SWOT Analysis

A SWOT analysis is designed to assess a company's strengths, weaknesses, market opportunities, and threats. The analysis provides valuable insight into market position, potential for growth, and possible issues to help you be sure as *hell* about your business. A SWOT analysis also reveals facts about your business, your competitors, and the current business climate. In the competitive world of ecommerce, an analysis of your strengths and weaknesses can help you determine your position in the industry. This also uncovers potential opportunities and threats presented by the competition, the market, the environment, and any other potential risks.

Doing a SWOT analysis on your competition helps bring to light other company's faults and shortcomings. When you have completed a SWOT analysis on your competitor, however, you also need to do one for yourself. This is not quite as easy, because you need to rank yourself against every weakness that you found your competitors to have. You must be completely honest in your assessment of your strengths and weaknesses for accurate results. If you can do this exercise with sincere effort and be sure as *hell* you have arrived at the hard truth, you will be on your way to finding solutions to fix the issues that could lead to Ecom Hell.

So, use the information that follows to perform a SWOT analysis for your company and then a separate one for your competitors. Put the analyses side by side and determine similarities and differences.

Strengths

Strengths represent the positive aspects of a business that add value and give a company the competitive advantage. Answer the following questions to determine the positive attributes of the business organization.

- What does the company specialize in?
- What resources (exclusive suppliers, high-tech staff) are available?
- What is cool and interesting about the company website?
- What advantages do your competitors have? What advantages do you have? Evaluate these advantages according to different criteria, such as superior product, customer service, marketing, and so on.
- Do they or you have first mover advantage?

Weaknesses

Weaknesses are the negative aspects of a business that diminish the value proposition and that place the company at a competitive disadvantage. Assess the controllable factors that hinder a company from gaining or maintaining a competitive edge (be honest when identifying your own weaknesses to make your SWOT relevant). Weakness needs to be dealt with head on, not covered up. Covering up weaknesses will only come back to haunt you and push you closer to hell

- Are the resources enough to sustain a business?
- Is there sufficient access to technology or skills?
- Is the customer service extraordinarily good, poor, or somewhere in between?
- Which areas need improvement?
- What is missing from the website?
- Who are your indirect competitors? What items do they sell that be can substituted for the ones you sell?
- Is the business easy to get into? – Easy barrier to entry

Opportunities

Opportunities are factors outside a business that help lead to success (opportunities identified as being internal to a business should be classified as strengths). Assess the external factors responsible for sustaining and growing a business.

- What opportunities exist in the market that can be capitalized upon (for example, a major competitor closes or ceases production or new laws come into effect)?
- Is it possible to tap into a new emerging market to grow the business?
- Are any new industry developments relevant to the business?

Threats

Threats are external in the sense that a company has no control over them. Your SWOT analysis will enable you to formulate contingency plans to counter these threats should they occur. Identify the factors beyond a company's control that place a business at risk. Classify every threat according to immediate consequences and the likelihood of each one happening.

- What factors (competitors, alternative products, etc.) can negatively affect the business?
- Has there been an obvious change in consumer behavior?
- Is there a developing trend that can render a product or service obsolete (e.g., cell phones eliminating the pay phone)?
- What situations threaten the company's marketing strategy?
- Once you've completed your SWOT, return to your business plan and update it accordingly. I know you are probably rolling your eyes right now, but continuing to flesh out your business plan is imperative, even if you create a simple one.

Other Questions to Ask When Sizing Up Your Competitors

- What are the top websites for the keyword you will be optimizing for?
- Can you track how much your competitors are spending on their marketing campaigns? Checkout Ispionage.com as a competitive tool.
- How does their website compare to yours?
- What kind of search engine optimization (SEO) strategy might they be employing?

You can use many of the checklists and tips in this book to benchmark your competitors' websites and business practices. This way, you can easily compare your business with theirs and determine at the minimum what you need to do to compete effectively. As significant as keeping tabs on your competition is, taking action on what you can influence and what you have control over, that is, your environment, is even more important. So, focus the majority of your business hours on your business instead of worrying about what the competition is doing to you. Then you will become a leader instead of a follower. And even if someone you would have followed ends up in *hell*, you will not.

Your Homework

1. Do a SWOT analysis on your potential competitors.
2. Do a SWOT analysis on yourself and your company.
3. Decide whether you are going to test the market by being an affiliate first before diving into the industry.

Section II.

Getting Started on the Right Road

Chapter 7.

Setting Up Your Business for Better than A Snowball's Chance in Hell

You will labor in Ecom Hell if: *you are not willing to work very hard and do whatever it takes.*

Because of the ecommerce myths I encounter, I want to reiterate to you that setting up your ecommerce business is no stroll through the park. Hard work is essential for any business to succeed. If you are like most entrepreneurs starting out, chances are you will be the only man/woman standing, the backbone of your business, with no one to rely on but yourself.

The Boss from Hell

Although you might not know this yet, you will become your worst boss and be forced to deal with inner moral conflicts that could be due to the constant hounding of your employees. If you are devoted, you will also become your best worker, being the first to start and the last to finish. Unless you are willing to swim through storms thick and thin, you might want to reconsider setting up your own ecommerce business. Make certain you are both mentally and physically prepared to straddle and mount the great workload ahead of you.

Domain Name

A domain name is not only your website's address (uniform resource locator or URL); it will also become your brand name online as you develop your business. Register a domain name that fits your product category and business image. Ideally, a domain name should contain words that describe your business, as this is beneficial to customers and search engines alike. Most businesses go with .com as their extension (as this is most appropriate to ecommerce stores).

Once you have positively decided on your Internet name, consider reserving a .net and .biz name the same as the .com name you chose. You might also buy the plural and singular forms of your domain names and any common misspellings. That way, no matter what customers type in, as long as it's close, they should find their way to your site. Keep in mind that a shorter domain name is easier to remember. In addition, when you have to give your email to your customers or vendors, long email names are a nuisance to type out.

Fitting your keyword(s) into your domain name (e.g., myweddingfavor. com) can be beneficial. However, this could be limiting later on, so you might want to opt for a more general domain, such as americanbridal.com, which covers a broader range within the wedding space but not as keyword targeted. You might want to do this if you think you will expand your business from offering just wedding favors to providing things like accessories and so forth. (We'll discuss this further later.)

Unfortunately, your choices might be limited because the domain name you want is already taken. You can check a domain's availability at just about any domain registration site. So let's get creative.

While you are registering for your domain name, you will want to select a hosting plan that provides the bandwidth and disk space you need. You can usually register your domain and host the website with the same vendor (GoDaddy, Network Solutions, etc). Choose either shared or dedicated hosting. Or you might want to start with a shared hosting environment and then move to dedicated hosting once your shop starts to grow and requires more space.

Keep It Short and Simple

Long domain names are difficult to remember and have a higher chance of being misspelled or mistyped by prospects. Why make it hard for someone to find you online or to remember your name from an advertisement? Choose a name that is memorable and resonates with your audience. Can you imagine if the founder of Amazon.com had chosen to name his company after the largest river in North America (the Mississippi) instead of the largest river in South America? Not only is Amazon more memorable, that river is infinitely easier to spell!

Combine Words and Phrases

Because domain names using common words are frequently unavailable— that is, someone else already owns the domain—you might want to opt for alternate spellings or even commonly used slang or foreign terms for your keyword. Zappos.com, which comes from the Spanish word for shoes, *zapatos*, is a great example.

Use Nonsense or Made-Up Words

Thankfully, on the Internet, names do not need to be actual words. Made-up words can just as easily convey your brand (Yahoo!, Facebook, YouTube, etc) and are more likely to be available.

Buy a Domain Name That Already Exists

If the only name you really want is already spoken for, you can make an offer to obtain a domain name from the current owner, for a fee. Many people have bought up names in the hopes of selling them. Check and see if the name is an actual website or a "parked" or "reserved" name. Some will have no website for the name, and others might have a generic redirect site that only lists other sites. After a few searches, you should be able to tell the difference.

Many domain name registration companies will act as your agent to help you through the process of acquiring the domain. Sometimes, a domain owner will advertise that the site is for sale, along with his or her contact info. Be careful not to spend more than you can afford just to buy the domain name. Remember that this is just the start of your ecommerce venture and that there are other expenses to consider.

Domain Name Checklist

☐ Two or three words (Try not to use hyphens if you can help it.)

☐ Look into old and expired domains.

☐ Research websites sitting on page 5 and up of a search to see if any of these sites are for sale.

☐ Register the most common misspelling for your domain name. Don't forget about the singular or plural version as well.

☐ Go to Facebook and Twitter to lock in your vanity URL (www. facebook.com/yourdomainname and twitter.com/yourdomainname). You might not need these right away, but you want to prevent anyone from using them. This applies to any social sites that you might want to use in the future.

Register your domain name with a company, such as GoDaddy, Network Solutions, or Yahoo!. Don't forget to add hosting, which is a separate charge from registering your domain.

Once you have decided on your domain name, secure a legal name for your company; this can be your domain name or another legal business name. If you choose the latter, you can set up a DBA (doing business as); for example, your legal name is XYZ Corporation, DBA: YourDomainName.

com. Once you secure your legal name, you can get a business license and incorporate.

There are a variety of ways to set up your business as a legal entity that will have tax and legal implications, so consult with an attorney and accountant on this step. If you choose to be a corporation, hold regular meetings with documented minutes as required by your state or laws in your location; otherwise, you might lose your corporate protection and take a surprise trip to Ecom Hell. You might also need to obtain a resale number in order to buy from wholesalers. (This is required in some states, such as California.) Go to your state government website to find out any legal requirements for setting up a business entity.

Double-check that you have the proper permits and forms for city, state, and federal levels. In the United States, you need a federal Employee ID Number (EIN) whether you are going to have employees or not. This is the number that will be used to identify your business for tax reasons. If you do become an employer, you will need to adhere to a host of laws regarding employers, such as displaying the proper workplace forms from the Occupational Health and Safety Administration and withholding payroll taxes.

Business Checklist

☐ Set up a business checking account.

☐ Obtain a resale number or state sales tax permit.

☐ Obtain a business license and/or incorporation and/or Federal EIN number.

☐ Assemble the necessary employee forms (see "Human Resources").

Setting Up Your Office/Warehouse Checklist

☐ Office furniture: desk, chairs, trash bins, recycle containers, lamps, etc

☐ Office equipment: fax machine or fax software, copier, scanner, printers, computers, monitors, telephones, shipping scale and shipping label printer (these might come free from your shipping partner, such as UPS), filing cabinets, etc

☐ Office supplies: stapler/staples, stamps, reams of paper (letter, legal), paper clips, tape, etc

☐ Shipping supplies: packing material (popcorn, peanuts), packing tape/gun, shipping labels, shipping boxes, etc

Your Homework

1. Set up shop, whether in a small office/warehouse or your home or garage.

2. Get your office/warehouse ready. For now, focus on the basics.

Business Plan Checklist

☐ Write down your business purpose, mission statement, core values, and business objectives.

☐ Business strategy: Define your critical success factors—that is, the key things your organization must do to be successful. What are you going to focus on to create happy customers and beat the competition?

☐ Business development: Who can help you, and where can you drum up business and sales?

☐ Business operations: What needs to be done, and how will it be done? Establish a tactical strategy plan and execution.

☐ Business finance: Create a budget. How much money are you putting in now? How much more money can you put in at a later time? How much revenue do you plan to bring in during the first twelve months? What expenses will you incur in the first twelve months? The next twenty-four months? The next thirty-six months? Plan your sales projections and burn rate.

☐ Create and document all business processes, job descriptions, and step-by-step procedures.

☐ Understand who your customers are going to be and how to go after them.

☐ Be vendor ready. Research where your competitors are sourcing their products (use my vendor questions checklist in the section on purchasing). Make sure you have enough vendors to provide a decent selection of goods. Before you start your business, establish at least two different sources of vendors. I once knew a guy who was nearly done with his ecommerce store design when his one and only supplier decided to retire. Needless to say, this left him stressed out and scrambling to find another vendor. In the end, he sold the finished store without ever getting a chance to launch his business.

Chapter 8.

Hell Hates Smart Technology

You will live in Ecom Hell if: *you are not willing to invest in technology.*

The days when business technology consisted of a phone, a fax machine, and a file cabinet are gone. In fact, soon, there will be few people around who even remember those times. Now business runs on technology, and an ecommerce business even more so than most. The right technology can be a great asset to your business. The wrong or inadequate tools can send you to Ecom Hell.

Many entrepreneurs, in an attempt to save money, choose a lesser technology solution that cannot grow with their business. This solution often locks them into a system that can potentially limit their business's growth. So, this is one of those situations where spending a little more money is wise, because you want a technology system that will guarantee stability and consistency for you and your business. Having the right technology can be a competitive advantage, look at Amazon. Of course, in order to choose the right technology, you have to know your long-term goals; that's right—you have to have a business plan. As I have said before, even an informal business plan is better than none at all.

Picking a technology platform that is perfect for your estore's requirements is crucial to your site's success. But with so many vendors offering ecommerce solutions (Yahoo! Store, Groove Commerce, Big Commerce, etc), choosing the best one can be tricky. Often, a cheaper "price tag" will win, but do not compromise reliability just to save a few bucks.

Choosing the right ecommerce vendor can take some time, and doing so is not as straightforward as relying on Google search results. If you are technical (i.e., a programmer), you'll have more options. If you are a nontechie, like me, go with the solution that has a lot of designers and developers who can support the system, as this will allow you to be pickier when choosing someone to build the site. The main thing is to get this right on the first try. So take your time and choose the best provider who fits your needs. Contact me if you want help with researching the right ecommerce platform for your business.

Picking an Ecommerce Platform

The front end of your website is what your customers see, so make it as inviting as possible (we will cover more on this in "Merchandising"). Generic template designs are a thing of the past. Most hosted ecommerce vendors now allow you to customize their templates or designs in any way. So look for a vendor who offers a solid selection of customizable templates that suit your design needs.

Large platforms like Yahoo! Small Business provide backup and redundancy, so there is no need for you to invest in your own servers. They also provide security from hackers and hosting support, so you don't need to hire an IT (information technology) person until your company gets bigger.

Mission-Critical Features

In addition to looking good, the ideal platform will have features that ensure front-end (shopping cart) and back-end (order processing, inventory management, and accounting software) compatibility. No matter how good a store looks to customers (front end), if everything is not functioning properly (back end), you are bound to disappoint visitors and there is a good chance you will be headed to…yes, that's right: Ecom Hell! Look for platforms that comply with the latest security (e.g., PCI compliance) to protect yourself from hackers.

Shopping carts should be compatible with your back-end system, merchant accounts, and payment gateway. Go with a company that has been around for a long time, so that you are not a guinea pig (beta tester). If you are just starting out, consider a hosted platform that provides a turnkey solution with a help desk and readily available customer support.

Some platform vendors integrate multichannel capabilities that allow you to sell products on Amazon, Google Merchant Center, and online shopping comparison sites. Even if you don't need them now, having these features integrated into your platform could come in handy in the future. Know what the total costs will be; ask if extra features are included or if there are additional fees.

I am not going to go into cross-channel selling, as you can always learn more about this selling strategy once your main ecommerce business is running smoothly. For now, I suggest you start small and simple.

The chances of getting everything you desire in an ecommerce platform without paying the price are very slim. Smaller ones run somewhere between $99 to $1,000 a month; mid-tier ecommerce platforms run about $2,000 to $12,000 a month; and enterprise versions may run up to $250,000 annually just to get started. The key is to understand how you are going to operate your business so you can afford most of the features you'll need. Personally, I like hosted solutions like Yahoo! Small Business, as they offer numerous developers and designers who can help with building out the site. This means you do not have the up-front investment of computer servers; in addition, there are fewer worries about up-time and more flexibility with website features and functionality.

Some owners move their website to another platform after a period of time but this is risky especially if your search engine ranking has been established. Therefore, it is very important that you select the right platform you can grow into so that the only reason that you are moving is that you've outgrown your platform and it's hindering your top line revenue growth.

51

Checklist for Platform Research

☐ Setup cost and monthly fees

☐ Wide selection of features and functions option for best ecommerce practices

☐ Third-party integration (i.e., with QuickBooks, inventory management software, customer relationship management software)

☐ Blog integration (e.g., Wordpress)

☐ Social media integration (e.g., Facebook, Pinterest, Twitter)

☐ Business-to-business (B2B) channel and multichannel support (e.g., eBay, Amazon)

☐ Comparison-shopping site integration (e.g., PriceGrabber, Nextag)

☐ SEO-friendly static pages

☐ Large community of third-party developers and webmasters that offer:

- Customizable website design
- Inventory management system
- Free 24/7 online and telephone support
- Forum community
- PCI-DSS compliant
- 99 percent up-time

Wish List for Platform Features and Functions

- Web analytics integration such as Google Analytics
- 99.9 percent up-time (read online forums regarding any complaints from other merchants)
- A large number (at least 1,500) of active merchants on its platform

- A large number of developers and designers supporting the platform
- Easy to learn and allows you to manage most features and functions, such as:
  - Adding and removing products
  - Managing rules, such as shipping charts and sales tax rates
- SEO-friendly website architecture
- Integration with order-processing and inventory software (back end)
- Integration with accounting software
- Blog platform integration (e.g., Wordpress)
- Offers coupons and single-use coupons, free gift with purchase, and/or gift cards/certificates
- Loyalty reward programs
- Cross-sell or upsell capability based on user-generated behavior
- Customer relationship management (CRM), such as call center tools (Built-in CRM is helpful in tracking customer data.)
- Option for merchandise return form to be done online with RMA # automatically assigned.
- Online chat
- Customer product reviews
- Internal search tool
- Mobile-optimized version (see "Mobile Commerce" for more info)
- Multiple image capabilities
- Multichannel sales (Amazon, eBay)
- Real-time inventory integration (removes out-of-stock items, etc)
- Registration (allows registration with open graph—ease of log-in)
- One-page checkout
- Sales tax management tools
- Management reporting tools such as sales and product filters. Most platforms have very poor reporting mechanisms, be sure you understand what is available to help you optimize your business.
- Shipping tools: free shipping, shipment segmented by weight (e.g., KingWeb Master's shipping manager)
- International shipment and currency payment options
- Ability for customers to easily update, cancel or change their orders before it's processed
- PCI compliant

- Payment options: credit cards, checks, PayPal, Google Check Wallet, BillMeLater.com, Wupay.com and Stripe
- Wish list and gift registry (let customer create lists)
- Web form ticketing system
- Website language translator
- Product video library
- Online shipping status tracking capabilities

Cool Website Features That Help Increase Conversion Rates

- Wish list
- Loyalty rewards program
- Coupons, Flash sales, Daily deals
- Customer testimonials
- Gift registries & Gift cards
- Enhanced search and navigation with faceted search, spell check
- Product-comparison tool
- Customizable checkout pages
- Cross-sell and auto-suggest tool (Yahoo! Small Business has this feature, and it rocks.)
- Personalization tool, such as Amazon's product recommendation, which is tailored to your click patterns and purchase history; can be combined with the cross-sell and auto-suggest tool
- Product reviews
- Question-and-answer feature that allows users/customers to interact with one another—This feature usually appears right on the product page, providing a social aspect by allowing user-generated content about the product.
- Persistent shopping cart—Allows the user to return to a shopping cart that has not been completed without having to go through the whole search process again
- Product availability (in stock)
- Product videos – look into Treepodia.com
- Multiple shipping addresses for the same order

- Auto-calculate free shipping when order qualifies
- Auto-populate coupons or promo information
- Show shipping cost calculator right on the product page (This will reduce your shopping cart abandonment rate.)
- Notification alerts—This is kind of like a personal shopper that alerts users of sales, coupons, products being added or going out of stock, etc.
- GEO targeting tools to help with marketing efforts

While we are on the topic of wish lists, here is a back-end checklist you can use to investigate back-end technology while you are still looking for a platform that works for you. I've used Stone Edge Order Manager combined with QuickBooks for our back-end. A good number of Yahoo! stores use Stone Edge as their back-end to manage their inventory and process their orders. One of your primary goal is to have a front-end as well as back-end link together to create an integrated customer experience.

I've worked out a special offer with Yahoo! Small business for saving on their platform when you sign up. Please "Call 866-781-9246 by December 31, 2014 and mention that you read this book to receive a special promotional offer on a new Yahoo! Store.

BigCommerce.com has over 36,000 business owners on their platform and I worked out a deal for an extended trial period. Go to this url: ecommsystems.bigcommerce.com

Back-End Checklist

☐ Shopping cart integration

☐ A back-end system that easily integrates with popular accounting software, such as QuickBooks or Peachtree Accounting

Ability to process orders or purchase orders in batches

☐ Custom or template emails for customers and vendors

- ☐ Supports multiple-store environment from invoices to packing slips to email

- ☐ Security setting for different users

- ☐ License for multiple workstations

- ☐ Barcode printing and scanning capability

- ☐ Automated merchandise return system

- ☐ Shipping scale integration

- ☐ Integration with popular shipping systems like UPS, FedEx, USPS, etc

- ☐ CRM system to log customer calls onto their orders

- ☐ Easily accessible by multiple departments to better understand customer demographic, purchase history, and purchasing patterns

- ☐ Supports kits and assemblies, including multilevel pricing and quantity discounts

- ☐ Robust inventory reporting, such as historical sales, popular items, dead stocks, etc

- ☐ Robust CRM that allows customer segmentation

- ☐ Custom and standard reporting capability—robust reporting tools

- ☐ Point-of-sale system for brick-and-mortar stores that integrates with your ecommerce platform

- ☐ Know the hard cost for your new technology—not just the cost to acquire it but also to maintain it

- [ ] Integration with popular email platforms

- [ ] Integrated with Multi-channel platforms like Ebay, Amazon and Buy. com

Mobile Commerce

Smart mobile devices, such as tablets, smart phones, and so on, are more prevalent than ever. As a result of what appears to be a permanent trend, mobile devices are quickly becoming a convenient way to browse and shop. As such, mobile commerce is expected to see sales growth of about 20 percent in some markets by 2014. Retailers are well aware of this fact and are constantly trying to figure out ways to turn casual browsers into ecommerce shoppers ready to make a purchase. The key to success via a mobile platform is to find a mobile commerce platform that works seamlessly with your ecommerce platform.

Be prepared and confirm that your mobile ecommerce store is ready to fulfill this demand for shop`ping on the go. As part of your research, make sure your platform provider is committed to mobile commerce. Even if you are not quite ready to use this feature, you want to know that you have options when the time is right, and hopefully that time is soon.

Benefits of Mobile Commerce

The obvious benefit of mobile commerce is that the customer can make a purchase from any location at any time. Customers do not have to go to a store physically or be at their desks. Even customers who prefer to pick up their items in person can complete the purchase online and have the item delivered to their local retailer; an email or text will notify them when the product arrives. Additional benefits of mobile commerce include the following:

- Easy access by customers with smart phones
- Convenience and time saving
- Customers are always connected
- Send very targeted marketing message

Cost of Starting a Mobile Commerce Site

The cost of starting a mobile commerce site can range from a few hundreds of dollars to thousands of dollars. The cost mainly depends on how "bulky" your current website is. If you have a lot of photos and graphics, that might not translate well to mobile devices. You might need to hire a web-design firm to streamline your existing website into something that can be easily accessed across all user devices. Or you can acquire the skills to do this yourself. Whichever option you choose, for your site to be mobile ready, it needs to:

- Contain web languages supported by the majority of the mobile market
- Have a simple design that allows mobile shoppers to browse, add items to their cart, and easily check out and complete their purchase
- Look into "responsive design" which means that depending on how the user comes into your website, the appearance of your website adjusts to their device of choice.
- Minimize the use of slideshows, preview images, live help, and other features likely to prevent your page from loading quickly on a mobile device

You also want to have a site that is compatible with as many mobile platforms as possible, because convenience promotes growth. At the minimum, confirm that your site works on the following:

- Android OS devices
- iOS: iPhone and iPod Touch
- Palm WebOS 1.4 and up (Pre and Pixi)
- BlackBerry OS 5 and up
- Windows Phone 6.5 and up

Getting the Most out of Mobile Commerce

Updates from Google Nexus and Apple include additional security features that make it easier for users to browse and select products and services from their mobile devices, whether a smart phone or a tablet. The key to getting the most out of mobile commerce is to:

- Make your product and service pages easy to read
- Set up a shopping cart that includes convenient payment links

- Make products easy to find
- Use a platform that supports secure credit card transactions

Although many people are using their mobile devices for purchases, the concept is new for others. In many cases, you have to overcome users' hesitations to get the most out of mobile commerce. This is not always an easy task.

One study found that web-enabled mobile device users are more likely to use their devices to check traffic, get news, check the weather, or find movie times than to buy products online. The more user-friendly and secure you make your purchase page, the more likely customers are to go ahead and complete their purchase while on the go.

Finally, make your website, including your social media efforts, as cohesive as possible. It remains unclear how mobile commerce fits into search engine rankings, but most experts agree that mobile commerce is going to continue to experience significant growth within the next decade.

Look into Fastpivot.com to see how they can help you integrate your mobile commerce with your social strategy.

Mobile Marketing

Take advantage of mobile marketing. These days, marketers are sending promotions and discounts to customers via mobile devices, such as phones, iPads, and so on. Consumers are spending more time on the mobile device than they are on the physical computer. Ensuring that all your marketing promotion work well on these type of device will help you reach your customer base and keep them connected with you. Keeping your marketing message simple is key. You may want to invest in having your ecommerce platform be mobile friendly at this juncture as more and more users are checking their emails in this manner. You'll want to make sure your mobile design is easy to navigate, omit banners and ad type images, show product images and short product description with an obvious add to cart button within the mobile screen size. Streamline your product category and only feature your crucial section as real estate space on mobile screen is at a premium.

Privacy and Security

While there are many benefits to making ecommerce transactions, privacy and security will always be a concern for consumers and retailers. Your sales growth will be limited if customers hesitate to complete a purchase because of security concerns. And if customers have concerns about making a purchase online, imagine their concerns about doing so via a mobile device. Perception is reality. Therefore, make customers aware that you have a secure site and that any data shared in a transaction is kept private, whether via computer or mobile device.

The full potential of ecommerce and mobile commerce depends on the availability of state-of-the-art technology and how fast businesses are able to incorporate updates in technology and security into their operations.

Your Homework

1. Simultaneously look for affordable but effective back-end and front-end systems. These systems must work together, so do this at the same time. Otherwise, you could discover that you have an affordable front-end platform that is not compatible with your back-end system.
2. Use the checklists and wish lists in this chapter to vet which system works best for you.
3. Determine which platforms your competitors are using. This should not be your deciding factor, but it helps to know what your competition is doing.

Chapter 9.

The Devil Is in the Details: Product Sourcing and Selection

You will experience Ecom Hell if: *you do not manage your inventory.*

Managing inventory is not complicated, but the devil is in the details and the work can be tedious, with tasks such as buying new inventory from vendors and placing reorders for out-of-stock items. In addition, managing inventory requires a bit of merchandising skill. There's always the chance you will get lucky and stumble upon the next hottest product, but you may also be unlucky and get caught on the downtrend, stuck with unsellable products.

Whatever the case, no one I know in the industry hit a home run every time with product selection. However, most experienced buyers make good choices; they understand their customers' needs, they make educated guesses, and they use analytics and historical data to help them make merchandising decisions. You can only make these things happen if you are willing to acquire the skill set needed to manage inventory properly and efficiently.

I recommend that you seek products with at least 40 percent up margins, meaning if it cost you ten dollars to make or buy, you can sell it for at least fourteen; of course, the higher the margin, the better. You will also want to have products that meet your average ticket cost of around fifty to seventy-five dollars, because this will at least cover your overhead per transaction. If you sell a lot of products at ten to thirty-five dollars each and if the average order is twenty dollars, you will find that this is a very hard way to make a living. You will barely break even, and you will have to sell truckloads of products just to eke out a living. Your goal is to be continuously increasing your average order value (AOV).

I do not recommend getting into a category with slim margins, as you can go broke trying to sell high volumes at low prices. Leave that to companies like Costco and Target, who can get away with making money selling low margin/high volume.

The Pricing Game

Many big retailers play pricing games with the MSRP and other MAP pricing. These prices are set up from the beginning (i.e., preprinted price tags from manufacturer) to set the higher retail price and allow margins for markdowns. I call it "the pretend retail price." They mark up the price so that they have wiggle room to mark it down for discount or to put it on sale. Have you ever wondered how things can be on sale for 50 percent off so frequently and these department stores are still in business? Most small retailers don't have the wiggle room; they may keystone markup (100 percent) and may be able to add an extra 20 percent padding to cover inbound shipping if the product can fetch the price that they are asking. In other words, they ask for what the market will bear. This is important to know because it will help you decide what product category you want to get into that may allow for this type of pricing structure. Always focus on value or even "perceived value" by your customers, and you should do well.

If you decide that you're going to compete on out-pricing your competitors, you may initially be able to sustain this strategy to capture market share, but you must know that it is only a temporary solution. It will not be your long-term solution as your competitors can also drop their prices and it will become a race to the bottom. Your goal, instead, should be to find a way to differentiate yourself and focus on building a better relationship with your customers for the long haul

When you have decided what you are going to sell, you need to find sources for your goods. You can find product suppliers through trade shows, importers, local sales representatives, and eBay. You can also sign up with a wholesale resource like WorldwideBrands.com. (I personally do not have any experience with them, but I have heard of many ecommerce businesses that use them as a resource tool.)

Knowing which questions to ask will help you get a better picture of how each supplier operates. Vendors come in a few forms: a direct source/ manufacturer, wholesaler, or distributor. Some suppliers also sell directly to consumers, thus making them your competition; ask whether your vendor has a retail channel (e.g., Amazon) or an online store.

Choosing Vendors

When researching vendors, maintain a vendor profile system with answers to each of the following questions for each potential supplier[2]:

- What product categories does the vendor sell?
- Who else purchases from the vendor (your competition online)?
- Does the vendor provide product images and descriptions? Is this information web-based or on a CD?
- How does the vendor want orders placed (by fax, email, electronic data interchange, XML feed, online data entry, phone, or some combination of the above)? Figure out which one best fits your process.
- Will the vendor help you create a product spreadsheet for you to upload on your site? These forms can streamline adding new items to your site, especially if you're short on staff. This extra service should be considered when selecting suppliers. (Be sure to rewrite the product descriptions.)

---

2 Note: This questionnaire will help you understand how best to incorporate the new vendor into your current process. (Some of the questions might not apply to drop-ship vendors.) Once you choose your vendors, have them fill out a W-9 form to ensure that they are a legitimate vendor, and issue a 1099 to each vendor at the end of each year.

- Does the vendor drop ship? If so, how do they charge for drop-ship fees: per item, per address/billing, or a flat fee?
- Does the vendor pad(charge extra) shipping charges? Can you use your own UPS or FedEx account?
- How does the vendor bill: per transaction or by monthly statement? Per transaction is usually preferred to match your purchase order (PO) issuance to their invoice.
- How does the vendor send the bill: by email or snail mail?
- What payment terms are being offered? Net 30? Net 15? Is there a discount if the invoice is paid within five to ten days?
- How does the vendor prefer to receive payment: by check or credit card?
- What is the vendor's policy for pricing: MAP (minimum advertised price) or MSRP (manufacturer's suggested retail price)? Do they enforce it?
- What is the vendor's back-order policy and process? Does the vendor ship back orders? What is the communication process to keep you informed of this?
- How does the vendor notify customers of out-of-stock or discontinued items or items that require product-description updates?
- What is the vendor's policy for damage claims for both drop ships and inventory items?
- What is the vendor's return and exchange policy?
- How many days from receipt of the purchase orders does the vendor ship? What is the cutoff time?
- Does the vendor offer blind shipping (for drop shippers)?
- What does the shipping label or paperwork look like? Can it be customized for your product? Does the vendor provide a customized packing list?
- How does the vendor send tracking numbers back to you? To the customer? Can the vendor provide text file transfer so that it can automatically go into your order management software? (Stone Edge Order Manager does this, and it saves a lot of time.)
- Does the vendor ship internationally? If so, how does the vendor charge for this? Is there a cap?

- Does the vendor provide real-time inventory updates? If so, is it done through a data feed? Does it link to your back end? What kind of back end does the vendor use?
- Does the vendor have purchasing dollar requirements? If so, is it per order or on an annual basis?

Additional Tips on Working with Vendors

- Beware of products that are sold as sets. Some vendors only sell products in sets, which is not a problem if you have a physical store, but it can wreak havoc for reordering.
- Before ordering from a vendor, find out how long the goods stay in the vendor's inventory. Are the products seasonal? Can they be reordered? How often are items discontinued? For example, with clothing, it might be hard to reorder once into the season, so you might want to order enough to carry through the season, especially if you find a lot of buzz about the product.
- Always check the goods when you receive them in your warehouse. Check them against the photo of the product on your website. Vendors sometimes change product runs, and things like color can vary from shipment to shipment. It's better to catch this as early as possible so that you are advertising what you have.
- Make sure you understand how the merchandise is packaged and how you will be receiving the goods. Some items are shipped bulk, which means you will have to buy boxes to put them into before shipping to customers (glassware and mugs are prime examples of items shipped bulk).
- If you make the option of gift boxes available, have plenty of gift boxes and other shipping boxes in stock.
- Always ask for discounts, such as wholesale discounts or volume discounts when buying case quantities.
- Once you've established a good relationship with suppliers (i.e., you have enough volume ordering), you may be able to piggyback your order with the vendor and get even better discounts and pricing. In this case, there are no holding costs or risks for the vendor because you take immediate delivery of the product; everybody wins.

- Some vendors ship goods third-day-air but charge you ground, which helps with just-in-time inventory so you're not overstocking products and taking up valuable warehouse space.
- Request to bill shipping to your own UPS or FedEx account. By consolidating shipping costs (inbound and outbound), you can earn greater discounts with freight companies and negotiate better rates on higher shipping volumes.
- Ask whether the vendor takes a credit card as payment. If possible, use your mileage cards to earn points. Then save these points for personal family vacations.
- If your product is perishable or consumable, create a reorder program.
- Before running promotions on specific products, either have them on hand or check that your vendors/drop shippers have them in stock to ship on your behalf.
- Creating bundles or bundling products together into "gift baskets" makes it harder to comparison shop and creates added-value for customers, because you've done the hard work of combining products that go together, thus making their gift unique.

Purchasing

Purchasing plays a crucial role in ecommerce. This department is responsible for all the business acquisitions, from computers and services to supplies and inventory. Its ability to analyze, negotiate, and buy is vital to an organization's success. As each vendor has its own way of doing business, this department should understand the different aspects of the vendors and how best to work with each. Purchasing's goals are to forge relationships with the best vendors in order to get the most value for the organization's dollar, without sacrificing quality, and to ensure timely deliveries and balanced inventory levels.

Questions that you will want to answer are: how much inventory value will you be holding at a given time period like monthly or quarterly if your business is seasonal? Other questions might be: when do you re-order and how often? Will you ship partial shipments or have your supplier ship on your behalf? What kind of pricing policy does your vendor enforce and do they give quantity or case discounts

One benefit from working with vendors who enforce MAP pricing is that generally their products are not discounted and therefore are more profitable.

A note of caution, I have come across websites who have built their entire business model based on procuring gray market goods or unauthorized resellers of particular goods. I highly discourage you to go into this direction. The 2 biggest problem that you will likely face is unreliable inventory sources and legal issues from the manufacturers or distributors.

Inventory Management Tips

- Understand your product margins. Have a margin keeper who watches your margin like a hawk.
- Know how much you need on hand to efficiently service your customers' orders.
- Review dead inventory stock frequently (*at least four times per year— more if you sell seasonal or holiday goods*).
- Review slow-moving inventory.
- Review damaged goods, especially for problematic packaging.
- Always know how your supplier is packaging the inventory.
- Make sure your inventory system has good historical data to help you with a reordering plan.
- Understand what products are easily substituted for another.
- Do review your website log reports or analytics for products frequently viewed with little sales information.
- Know what your best sellers are.
- Make a deal with your suppliers when you know they are close to discontinuing an item. Buy it all. If you don't have the warehouse space, make a deal for them to rent you some space or store it for a while. This works for drop shippers too. The key is to own the supply and not let your competitors have any stock. Be careful, as your competitor might be using a similar strategy.

- Inventory data entry is one of the most laborious and detailed tasks that purchasing managers or buyers have to do. Incorporate an ongoing strategy for this task; do not leave it as something you do two or three times a year. In my previous company, we were always on the lookout for new products, and we added new items all year round. This allowed us to have fresh content while also keeping our website interesting and giving customers a reason to keep coming back.
- Ship old items first. Be aware of expiration dates, products that include batteries, and so forth.
- Create a quality-control process. Who will check incoming goods for quality? Who will match the actual product against the photo and description provided on the website?

Working with Drop Shippers

Drop shipping sends goods directly from the supplier to your customer. An advantage of drop shipping is this enables you to focus on marketing your products and developing your website and to worry less about shipping, warehousing, and fulfillment. However, the disadvantages of using a drop shipper might outweigh these benefits. For one thing, you lose control over the shipping process, and customers may experience delays in resolving issues, such as late shipments and returns. In addition, you lose the confidentiality of your customer list.

You might have to deal with a drop shipper who also ships for many other stores, including your competition. Since drop shippers have reduced the barrier to entry, many stores are drop shipping, even big stores like Macy's, Kohl's, and Walmart. Because of low margin, it's harder to turn a profit using the pay-per-click model.

Most drop shippers provide blind labels and charge a markup on shipping. So, select products that are still profitable, even after all the fees, shipping costs, and handling charges. Drop shipping can quickly erode your profits. If the product is not profitable, stay away; it does not make sense to spend marketing dollars to attract visitors to make purchases on products that are not profitable. You might also want to request that the drop shipper use your UPS number to avoid their markups. They also often charge a drop-ship fee. You usually pay the invoice once the product ships, or the drop shipper could charge your credit card on file.

As your company grows, explore third-party providers like Vendornet. com, which can help you manage your ever-growing paperwork.

In my previous company, we operated a hybrid model in which 35 percent of our products were drop shipped and 65 percent were stocked goods. It's pretty difficult to completely inventory everything in your warehouse; it increases your holding costs, your financial risk, your warehouse space, your number of employees, etc.

When Drop Shipping Makes Sense for You

- If you have inventory that is high volume, low-dollar value, high turnover, and/or heavy to ship, it makes sense for it to go directly from your vendor to your customer, without coming to you first. It is especially helpful if your vendor is centrally located in the middle of the country.
- Your vendor's shipping distance to most customers is within three days. My company is on the West Coast. If you receive an order from the East Coast and that's where your vendor is, have them drop ship for you. The time and cost to receive a shipment and turn it around erodes profits and adds on extra shipping costs.
- If you are testing new product ideas, it's a good idea to use a drop shipper first. This way, you can see if there is demand for the goods; when volume goes up, you can source the goods and bring it in-house, thus reducing exposure to warehousing products that don't sell. It also allows you to offer a broader selection of products.
- Using a drop shipper can help with managing cash flow. If you're short on capital, drop shipping is a viable option to get you started and help you discover which niche of product mix you should ultimately focus on.

Some Cautions to Be Aware of When It Comes to a Drop-Shipping Model:

- There is more competition in drop shipping, because it has reduced the barrier to entry. Products are a commodity and seemingly found everywhere.
- You have less control. Since goods are coming out of someone else's warehouse, you have less influence on the process. You can't include marketing material. You don't get to choose the boxes or packing material they use. For example, imagine you sell "green" products, but your vendor packs the item with Styrofoam peanuts. This is less than congruent and can ultimately hurt your brand.
- Your drop shipper might not take returns, so you could end up with unwanted product at your warehouse.
- If there are customer service issues, such as damaged goods or replacements, there is a little more hassle to factor in. But it's nothing that a good agreement and a keen understanding of your vendor's process can't resolve.
- Paperwork! If you're being billed per shipment, then you still have to enter these into your system, even if the vendor charged your credit card. You'll also need to reconcile these against your credit card statements to ensure that you were charged correctly.
- It can be labor intensive. If you or your vendor does not have an automated process, you might have to enter each order manually into their back end, which can be very time-consuming and more prone to human error.
- Your drop shipper might go out of business, leaving you unable to fulfill your customers' orders.
- Your drop shipper might not be able to provide you with tracking numbers to your shipment, which will often result in more customer service calls from your customers.
- If you have more than one website and you're using the same drop-ship vendor, there could be some confusion over billing and shipping orders to customers.
- Some drop shippers have their own retail sites or sell on Amazon Marketplace and eBay. Become familiar with their pricing structure as well as their marketing promotions. I once had a drop shipper

with multiple retail websites who was discounting their goods and offering free shipping. It was difficult to compete with them on their products.

- You don't have real time data to their inventory level, so you might sell a product that is actually out of stock.
- Drop-shipping fees and shipping cost can erode your profit margins.

Merchandising Your Store

Within your market, learn about your customers, including their income, education, gender, and marital status. What does this demographic like to purchase, and how do they spend money and use products? You can learn more about demographic information by contacting a related industry magazine for their media kit. These magazines often have quite a bit of information on the same customer base you are targeting. The more you know about your customer, the better you will understand the relationship between your sales strategy and product selection and which types of vendors work best.

Your product images and descriptions, as well as the overall look and feel of the website, must be user-friendly and appropriate. Getting this right will determine whether your store is profitable or you take a trip... you know where! Visit local retail stores, especially the trendier ones, to get new and interesting product ideas. Always be looking out for product ideas when you travel or attend trade shows.

Merchandising for Conversions

Traditional stores have sales staff to "sell" features and benefits, but selling online means educating your audience (that is, teaching consumption). To effectively educate an audience, you need to provide great product information, including photos showing the product in use, usage ideas, and how-to-type advice (for example, how to get the most out of the product, how to save money using a product, etc). This education can be provided in the form of videos, copywriting, articles, and tutorials, to name a few options.

Thanks to technological advances and the social web, merchants have more and more ways to tap into product videos, customer product reviews, and ratings to help influence consumers' buying decisions. You will learn more about this phenomenon in the affiliate-marketing and social-media-marketing sections of this book.

Checklist for Merchandising Your Store

☐ Carry products with different price points.

☐ Offer a broad product assortment/selection that appeals to different tastes (e.g., offer several color options).

☐ Provide great product images from different angles.

☐ Provide great product videos, including how-to videos.

☐ Offer a large selection, but not too much that it's overwhelming (at least twelve to eighteen per product category is my recommendation).

☐ Try to stay away from products sold to major discounters.

☐ Work with vendors to create a product that is exclusive to your site.

☐ Carry local designers and boutique brands that are not sold everywhere online and are hard to find in retail stores.

☐ Put each product into multiple categories in your web store whenever possible.

Packaging

A quick note about packaging: Some suppliers and importers have very generic black boxes or (even worse) factory-issue brown boxes. When customers spend lots of money on your product, there is a certain expectation that the product is going to arrive in a presentable manner. If products arrive at your warehouse in less-than-appealing packaging, either work out something with the vendor to provide better packaging or decide whether you're willing and able to repackage the goods before sending them to the customer.

If you are willing to repackage the goods, you will incur an up-front investment in boxes, labels, and labor. You will need to tag the products with the correct barcode (if you use this system) or attach a stock-keeping unit (SKU) sticker (inventory number) to help identify the product for storage and shipping.

Ugly packaging gives a low-quality vibe. Whether or not this vibe is valid, first impressions and perceptions make a world of difference in having a final sale versus a product being returned for a refund. However, some retailers are now giving consumers the option of being more environmentally friendly and agreeing to orders without the nicer packaging. You will have to do some research and test this idea to see if this is a good fit for your customer base.

Your Homework

1. Decide how much inventory you're going to carry. How much will be stocked? What will be drop-shipped by your vendors?
2. Write out the steps and procedure on how to place orders with your vendors for drop shipping.
3. Write out the steps and procedures on how to place orders with your vendors for stocked items.
4. Create a vendor profile for each vendor.
5. Prepare items that you would like to order. Review and verify all product margins, and get product photos and descriptions from vendors.

Chapter 10.

Building Your Online Store

You will face Ecom Hell if: *you cannot take criticism.*

Your most unhappy customers are your greatest source of learning.

—Bill Gates

Many of us can be a little too sensitive when it comes to dealing with criticism of our work. We take others' comments personally, often feeling as if we have been attacked rather than assisted. But not all criticism is bad. When you receive criticism about your online store, for example, you can learn a great deal from customer and expert feedback on how to improve the usability and conversion of your website features and layout. Over the lifetime of your website, you will receive criticism, whether from customers, employees, or usability experts. You must be willing to listen to their suggestions and even test their ideas.

Consider the Customer's Experience

Your website should be designed with your target audience in mind. Regardless of your niche, focus on a clean, simple navigational design and a professional-looking site. Good navigation will reward you with higher conversion of visitors to customers. Avoid clutter that could confuse your visitors and cause them to shop elsewhere. If customers cannot quickly and easily find what they are looking for on your site, you will likely lose the sale and might eventually take a trip to…by now you know where.

A well-designed website prioritizes customers' needs (to find items quickly) and provides multiple ways to get to the same content (i.e., through category navigation and internal site search).

Write website content for your customers, using a tone and lingo that resonate with your audience. Do not make your customers work at getting things accomplished. Use legible fonts that are appropriate for your audience (e.g., use a larger font size for Baby Boomers). Usability is key; everything a customer needs to do on your site should be intuitive and easy to figure out. Can your website pass the mom test? That is, is your site easy enough for a distracted, multitasking mother to find what she wants and buy from you while tending to small children and trying to find her credit card all at the same time?

Best Practices Checklist for Enhancing Customers' Experience with Your Website

☐ Provide clean, consistent navigation. Avoid clutter, use consistent messaging and good grammar, and provide interesting content for readers.

☐ Design a professional-looking site. This can make your business look bigger than it is, which can create trust. (Visitors will want to give you the benefit of the doubt.) Visitors need to trust the website in order to become customers.

☐ Use consistent, attractive colors appropriate to your product and industry—and no background music please!

☐ Include quality product images, good use of multiple images, and an image-enlarging feature.

☐ Create a professional-looking, memorable company logo and tagline.

☐ Make sure the site is easily scannable (i.e., can be taken in at a quick glance). This inspires visitors to stay and browse.

☐ Anticipate your customers' needs even before they know they need or want something.

☐ Design an intuitive layout that doesn't make customers work hard to find what they want.

☐ Build a site that is fast loading. Optimize your images, and externalize your scripts so that your website site loads quickly, without delay while the behind-the-scenes information fully loads.

☐ Verify that all links are working properly and take users to the correct destinations. Do this weekly.

☐ Respond promptly to customer inquiries.

☐ Provide authentic customer product reviews and company feedback.

☐ Test your product pages to see how well they convert.

Home Page

Your home page is the public face of your business. It's the most visited page of your website, and as such, it needs to grab visitors' attention in eight seconds or fewer. Most ecommerce store owners struggle with this; they often make the mistake of cluttering the home page with too many products, trying to dump every bit of information on that first page. A busy home page without good navigation can scare visitors away and reduce overall site conversion.

Think of the last time you clicked on a link that sent you to a badly designed or cheap-looking site. Did you stay and give it a chance, or did you simply click on the next search result?

Help your visitors by focusing on what you want them to do on your home page. Ensure that all links you want them to click on are obvious and that anything important, like email opt-ins, is visible and above the fold.

The bottom line when considering a website's aesthetic is to make sure whatever you choose appeals to your target customer and that your site is tasteful. Ideally, the colors you use on your website should mirror those in your logo and your brand's color scheme. Likewise, the images should convey your store's products or services and, most importantly, your value proposition.

Determine the most vital information you want your visitors to know about your company. Your home page needs to explain clearly what your company does and how it solves the visitor's problem or fulfills his or her needs. If you are selling products, categorize products so they can be easily found from the home page.

From your home page, visitors should be able to find what they are looking for in three clicks or less. One way to achieve this is by ensuring that your navigational structure is logical and user-friendly. Write naturally, using keywords with which your customers are familiar. The key is to provide good content for your visitors.

You might also want to include your company's value proposition.

- Why should people buy from you?
- What's in it for them?
- And why should they trust your site?

Focus on the benefits for the visitor rather than on why you are the best or your competitor is not; gain visitors' trust by having useful and helpful content, pleasing graphics and photos, and a professional-looking site.

You might additionally want to "borrow" trust by using trust seals. Such seals and logos, like those from Trust-Guard.com, Trustee, or the Better Business Bureau (BBB), can help increase confidence in your site. If nothing else, borrow brand trust by placing logos of the credit cards you accept (Visa, MasterCard, AMEX) above the fold. Use these logos strategically, however; do not overdo it, or your site will contain a sea of seals.

The internal site search feature or search box on the home page is one of the most frequently used features on an ecommerce site, yet it is largely overlooked by e-tailers. Help visitors save time by installing an effective search tool so they can quickly find what they need. Ensure that your search box is above the fold and large enough that visitors can find and use it. Test your search box to ensure everything works properly and produces good results, even if an item is incorrectly spelled. Later, I share with you how to use site search data to improve your conversions.

In addition, be sure that the design of your footer area (the bottom of your page that shows up on every page of your site) is scannable.

Other pages that should have easy-to-access links from your home page include the following:

- About us—Customers feel more at ease when they have a sense of whom they are doing business with. Include a story about why you started the site. Show pictures of yourself, your staff, and your office/building to humanize the online shopping experience and to connect with your customers.
- Contact us—Many ecommerce sites fail to include contact information, such as a (toll-free) phone number, fax number, email address, and physical address. "I do not want the customer to call" is not only a poor excuse but also a missed opportunity to engage customers. With every call, your company has a chance to get to know its customer better, helping you formulate customer-centric policies that translate into better customer service. It's also a good idea to provide a way for customers to leave feedback about your site and your product or service. An email opt-in field, where visitors who like your site can subscribe to your email-marketing database, is another great contact tool. Instead of using a catchall email account, provide a contact form with a drop-down menu so customers can choose the appropriate person or department.
- FAQ—Provide a question-and-answer section that addresses the most common concerns or questions customers might have or ask.

- Customer Service Pages: Includes shipping options and cost. How to use your website if there are technical requirements or even how to fill out purchase options for products. Don't forget to provide details on how to return products to your warehouse.
- Privacy policy—In addition to having a separate privacy policy page, you might want to display this prominently on your top navigation or footer area. Most websites and merchant providers will not let you go live without a visible privacy policy in place.

Home Page Do's

- Striking "hero shot" (best photo representation of your website)
- Toll-free (800) phone number and email address link clearly visible on every page
- Live chat option
- Appealing logo
- Visible search box
- Appropriate tagline that sums up what the site is about
- Sensible navigation bar on the left side and top of each page
- Featured products
- Graphics to funnel visitors into the interior pages
- Clean, uncluttered graphics and design
- Clear call to action: buy something or subscribe to our newsletter
- Legible, easy-to-read fonts and colors
- Trust seals/logos
- Site bread crumbs

Home Page Don'ts

- Don't test visitors' patience and short attention spans with a slow-loading site. Slow sites inevitably hurt your SEO rankings. The best way to optimize for speed is to reduce the file sizes of your images and to ensure that your coding is clean and the files externalized.

- Don't have broken links. Make sure that all links are working and are taking visitors to the correct pages.
- Don't use annoying pop-ups.
- Don't require registration or sign up just to enter the site. (However, registration is OK after a customer has already shopped.)
- Don't hijack a visitor's browser by immobilizing the back button.
- Don't use small font sizes. Baby Boomers are aging now, so don't make your fonts so small that they are a strain to read on LCD monitors.

Category Pages

As much as possible and whenever possible, lead your visitors from your home page to your category page via the sales funnel.

The Depth and Breadth of Your Category and Inventory Selection

There is a widespread webmaster obsession with the home page, but the category pages are where you will see your conversion increase, with less bounce rate. The category page is where customers can find the products they are looking for. Be sure to feature your most profitable and most popular categories prominently. As on the home page, help visitors by making navigation effortless and intuitive (the fewer clicks away, the better). If you want someone to make a purchase from a page, make sure that the "add to cart" buttons are obvious and clearly marked.

Optimize your category pages with key elements and images that let visitors know they are in the right place for the items they want. If you have a lot of products, you may need a subcategory page or maybe even a sub-subcategory page. But bear in mind that the more clicks away, the more likely the chance that you will lose your visitors' interest.

Example:

Home page --> Category Page (Wedding Favors) --> Subcategory (Fall Wedding Favors) --> Product Page (Fall Candle Wedding Favors)

Category Page Checklist

☐ Sort products by best sellers, price, customer review, color, manufacturer, etc.

☐ Break out items into several pages, as too many items on one page can be overwhelming. However, be sure to have a "view all" option as well.

☐ Include SEO-friendly and appropriate content.

☐ Include product review icons

☐ Include two or three category page deep, any more is confusing.

☐ Create a product comparison option where visitors can compare products to discern distinctive differences. This also is a great conversion tool.

☐ Show relevant banners above the products—lets users know that they're in the right section.

☐ Include promotional icons when applicable (e.g., New, Sale, Play Video)

Product Pages

Effective product descriptions are not just sprinkled with keywords; more important, they use emotional trigger words that relate to how the user will engage or interact with the product once acquired. Emotion creates motion, and the motion you are after is your visitor turning into a customer by making a purchase.

Tie product benefits with emotional anchors that your visitors can relate to. For example, what emotions would a user have by owning a Rolex watch? *Pride, importance, wealth, success, accomplishment*—all of these are emotional trigger words.

Good-quality product photos and detailed product descriptions are critical to selling online, because the buyer cannot touch and feel your goods. Show products in all colors. If a sweater comes in five colors, enable the customer to view the same item in any of the five colors. Post multiple product images to show the front, back, and any other orientation a customer might want to view.

Enable a zoom feature for photos to showcase fine details that may not be readily apparent. Show scale by posting photos in different situations. For example, if you are selling handbags, include photos of a petite and a tall woman carrying the same purse.

Watermark your images with your logo or copyright information so others can't use the images without your permission. But be careful—if you want to use these photos for other sites in the future, plan accordingly.

At the bottom of each page, include thumbnails (a smaller version of a product photo) of complementary (upsell) items.

Product Page Tips

- Make sure your photo resolution is 72 dpi. Any higher and your site's load time will be affected.
- The click-to-enlarge/zoom task should ideally open to at least a six-by-six-inch image.
- Ask vendors for multiple or exclusive photos. Only retake a photo if you can do better.
- Hire a professional, local photographer and work out a deal for ongoing work (fifteen to forty dollars a photo is reasonable).
- Rotate the image. Sometimes you can get away with a slight rotation that changes the perception of the image. This is one way to differentiate yourself from your competitors.
- Show different angles of each product.
- Remove the vendor's background from the photo, and add your own to match your site's color scheme.
- Leave out images of products you do not sell, as this will lead to confusion, disappointment, or dissatisfaction.

- Before placing an order with a vendor, make sure you know how you are going to photograph, display, and sell the product (bundled with other items, two-for-one, etc).

- Know what kinds of promotions you can offer and what kinds of similar products you can cross-sell or upsell.

- Some vendors have sampling programs that enable you to get free or loaner samples for product photo shoots. If they are loaners, you just need to return them in their original condition. Some vendors discount sample or display models that you can purchase.

- When offering discounts, make sure the discount is reflected in the shopping cart, with an obvious minus (not plus) symbol to eliminate the potential for confusion.

- Rewrite product descriptions from the vendor (150- to 300-word descriptions are optimal). Make sure you're updating unique content that incorporates keywords, keyword phrases, and emotional trigger words that highlight the benefits of your product. Hiring a contract writer will keep you from sounding like the rest of the competition and will create a unique personality for your store. Also, we had good luck with Elance.com in finding a US-based writer who understood the domestic demographics better than a foreign-based writer would. The reason for writing new description is to avoid duplicate-content penalty imposed by the search engine if your content is the same as other websites.

- A "related items" feature is an easy way to cross-sell and upsell. Make sure the products are truly related or true alternative options to the product being viewed, as you don't want to cannibalize your own sales.

- Include multiple "add to cart" locations, as this can help with increasing your conversion rate.

- Once you learn which products are selling and you are able to replenish them frequently, include a "best-seller" icon on the product image.

- When products are new or just added to your site, include a "new" icon on product images.

- Include social widgets for easy sharing, like on Facebook and Pinterest.

- "Frequently purchased together" options are great tools to help increase order value.
- Create question-and-answer lists for each product. Customers can read this to get insight on products. If your customer service department or live chat log is always getting asked the same question, you can add FAQs to your product description page. These lists also help with conversion and SEO content.
- Include in-house product reviews, such as video reviews or written reviews, to help visitors decide which product is best for them.
- Include alternative text (alt text) for each product image.
- Use bullet points to highlight benefits and product features so visitors scan content faster.
- Ensure that the "click to enlarge image" option really does provide a larger image than is normally shown as the default product image size.

Product Page Checklist

☐ Provide cross sells and up sells.

☐ Show customer testimonials and product reviews.

☐ Use multiple images to display different angles.

☐ Provide product videos, perhaps on YouTube. Display the videos near the main image, and always brand your videos.

☐ Include the product name, price, and item number.

☐ Include shipping cost and shipping options to reduce shopping cart abandonment.

☐ Include helpful icons, such as "sale" or "new," when applicable.

☐ Provide SEO-friendly product descriptions with complete details.

- [ ] Include shipping delivery information and options, a shipping calculator, and an arrival estimator.

- [ ] Provide social-media widgets and trust seals, awards, and recognitions.

- [ ] Include stock availability.

- [ ] Provide tier pricing, if applicable.

- [ ] Create a visible and attractive add-to-cart / buy button.

- [ ] Add it all feature – very useful if you sell items that are part of a collection like beddings.

Tiered Discount Offering

One of the proven pricing strategies that merchants have used to increase income and margins is to upsell to an existing customer. You already have a captive shopper, so why not reward his or her spending by offering tiered discounts. In fact, giving this type of discount is often less expensive than getting a new customer (how much was spent in marketing dollars to attract a converting customer). Tiered or multiple-item-purchase discounting works well with regular customers and bargain hunters. Make this discount program obvious, with clear information on your site.

Shopping Cart and Checkout Page

Your shopping cart is the most critical element of your ecommerce site. This is where customers select products they wish to purchase, give you their personal data, and choose and pay for shipping. At this point, you can ask customers to register (create a customer profile), or you can keep this step simple (asking people to fill out too many questions might scare them into abandoning the shopping cart and failing to complete the sale process). Include a thank-you page that appears right after a customer places an order. Let customers know that they should be receiving an order confirmation via email. Ask them to add your company email address to their contacts so that your mail does not go into their spam folder.

Also let customers know the company name that will appear on their credit card bill. This is especially imperative if your website is a DBA of the name on the merchant account (with which your customer is most likely not familiar). This simple step will save a lot of confusion and unnecessary chargebacks from your merchant processor.

PCI Compliance

Shopping carts act as a front end for online stores, passing secured information to a payment gateway. Review the gateway services supported by your software before acquiring the shopping carts. Avoid credit card fraud, and protect your customers' credit card information by making sure that your gateway provider complies with the Payment Card Industry Data Security Standard (PCI DSS).

Shopping Cart Abandonment

Most websites suffer from shopping cart abandonment. The average percentage of abandoned shopping carts—that is, purchases that are begun but never completed—ranges from 59 percent to 80 percent. That sounds pretty high.

The challenge is to find out why people are not completing their orders and then work to improve this ratio. In many cases, visitors are trying to figure out what the shipping cost will be. I am a big advocate of showing shipping costs right up front in the product page. If your visitors know the shipping costs and shipping options, including when products will be delivered, before adding anything to the cart, your conversion rate will go up, your bounce rate will go down, and your shopping cart abandonment rate will be dramatically reduced.

One of my biggest pet peeves is a website that requires me to register just to find out what the shipping cost will be. If a site requires registration to shop, they had better give me lots of incentive to do so up front.

Most shopping cart pages fail to do a good job letting customers know how to check out easily. If you are going to require registration in order to check out, make sure that that process is intuitive and easy to follow. An ecommerce best practice that will help with your conversion is to give visitors the option of checking out without registering or ask them to register after they have completed the purchase (get the money first). You also want to collect their email for future opportunities to sell to them.

The shopping cart page is a friction page, with lots of things to fill out. Your goal is to reduce the friction. I hate filling out forms. And to go through all that work of forms only to be scared off by a shipping cost frustrates me. So, find ways to reduce that friction.

Look at Amazon as an example. Amazon reduces friction in two key areas. First, they use the Amazon Prime program to give away free shipping, and they add value by offering two-day delivery. Second, they offer one-click shopping, thus removing the need to fill out so many forms each time a customer shops. All shipping, billing, and credit card information is already with Amazon after your first purchase, and that is why Amazon owns a significant share of the ecommerce business in the world. Both of these practices are excellent examples of incentives to register.

Shopping Cart Page Checklist

☐ Test a one- or two-page checkout layout (e.g., combine billing/shipping info). One-page checkout is ideal.

☐ Capture email information early on the page for your shopping cart abandonment email program.

☐ Only ask for absolutely necessary information.

☐ Display a coupon box only when certain criteria are met (e.g., if a customer comes to the site through affiliates or emails, etc). Otherwise, hide this option, if possible. If this is not possible (as is the case in most carts), then provide coupon code link to prevent customers from leaving the site to go look for it online.

☐ Take out clutter on the left navigation bar and minimize the top navigation bar.

☐ Provide an option to purchase and verify shipping charges without registration.

☐ Include a visible promotion header, if applicable.

☐ Offer a free shipping countdown tool (if you offer free shipping).

☐ Provide a shipping calculator on the product page if possible.

☐ Provide graphic steps for the checkout process.

☐ Include trust seals, but use them sparingly.

☐ Provide a telephone number for the option to phone in orders.

☐ Ensure that your SSL certificates are up-to-date.

☐ Set your default credit card to Visa, as there are more Visa users. For most customers, this will be one less step in the process. Then list the other cards in alphabetical order after that.

☐ Set up a persistent cart, which remembers each visitor's last entry and keeps it in tact until his or her next visit.

☐ Send order confirmation emails after each order is submitted and shipped.

Merchant Account

The majority of online sales are made through credit card payments. To accept Visa/MasterCard/Amex/Discover credit card payments and debit card payments, you will need to set up a merchant account with a merchant account provider. Address Verification System (AVS) and the CVV number help reduce the chances of accepting a stolen card. Make sure that these options are activated on your site to eliminate (or at least reduce) the number of fraudulent orders.

You will need your merchant ID (MID) and terminal ID (TID) numbers to put into your payment gateway. If you need additional help, speak to an account representative who can walk you through these easy steps.

Bear in mind that if you process or capture payments outside of your cart, you may need another separate account, such as Authorize.net for the back end.

Don't Underestimate Your Revenue Expectation

Merchant providers are suspicious of sudden bursts of business activities. If you expect your sales for the first month to be twenty-five thousand dollars, ask for fifty thousand, and then build your business to the next level. If your business is highly dependent on seasonality, you will want to notify your merchant account agent or representative. If you do get a call or are contacted by your merchant processor, respond promptly with an explanation to avoid a freeze on your account. I have a friend who had his deposits to his bank account frozen to the tune of fifty thousand dollars for several months because his business took off so fast that the credit card processing company raised a red flag on his account while they investigated. Needless to say, he was furious and stressed out about his cash-flow situation.

Understand Merchant Provider Fees and Rates

Be aware of any fees and rates that your provider requires. For instance, setup fees are charged for new accounts, though many providers do not charge this anymore. Chargeback fees, usually around twenty-five dollars per occurrence, are charged when a customer or issuing bank disputes a transaction, either because they do not recognize the transaction or it was a fraudulent charge.

The following three types of fees are also common:

- Transaction fees—A small charge for every transaction processed, usually thirty to fifty cents per transaction
- Discount fees—A percentage of monthly sales taken by the merchant account provider. Depending on the type of business, discount rates range from 1.5 to 5 percent.
- Monthly account fees—A flat fee paid each month for account-related services

In addition, there are various other fees you might encounter. Be wary of providers who offer suspiciously low rates. More often than not, they come with hidden fees.

Understanding how merchant accounts work will not only help you avoid problems; it will also allow you to maintain good business owner to merchant provider relations. To further strengthen good standing, avoid excessive chargebacks and selling products or services outside what you declared in the service agreement. I recommend that you use a merchant provider that works with several processors, so that you can figure out which program best fits your needs.

Alternative Payment Methods

PayPal and Google Wallet are alternative payment processing methods that allow customers to pay for goods using credit cards or a checking account without disclosing their banking information to you directly. Many customers prefer to make payments using one of these methods, so be sure you are set up to accept payment in this manner. Other payment type providers are WuPay.com and billmelater.com.

Merchant Account Checklist

☐ Deposit funds into your account within one to two days.

☐ Know the discount rate, transaction fee, and minimum fee.

☐ Know the qualified and nonqualified rates. These may be different for qualified cards, not qualified cards, reward- or loyalty-based cards, and so forth.

☐ Know the chargeback fees and the policy for reversing chargebacks.

☐ Coincide monthly cutoff dates with bank statements and credit card deposits.

☐ Aggregate fees into one monthly deduction instead of deducting per transaction.

☐ Ask your bank to start and end your statement cycle at the beginning of each month.

☐ Ask to have your monthly merchant fees deducted as a lump sum, as this will help make it easier to do monthly bank and merchant statement reconciliation.

☐ Know your credit card company's cutoff hours for batching daily sales. Coordinate this with your order processing to make it easier to match up funds deposited into your bank account daily.

Use a familiar or conventional ecommerce layout design. Using a less conventional look is riskier. However, if you have a unique model in which you can easily communicate to your customer base and they can easily tell their friends about it, then you might be onto something amazing.

Once you have finished building your estore, put your site to work for you!

Your Homework

Take notes on features and functions you like. Create a wish list, and sort by importance.

Chapter 11.

Web Designers and Developers

You experience Ecom Hell if: you do not have patience and understanding with web designers and developers.

Although most web designers and developers are pretty on top of their game, good ones are hard to find. Sometimes, you get unlucky and have to work with the busier ones, who are juggling multiple clients' demands and deadlines. To make life easier for you and your web designer or developer, make sure you are absolutely clear on what you want, as no one works well in the midst of confusion.

In addition to keeping things straightforward, be sure to listen to the designer or developer's advice. Most web designers and developers have gained great experience in creating websites and may have insight on what works best. But, remember, this is your store, and ultimately, you are responsible for making decisions on what is best for your company. If you do end up working with someone who is overtasked and always late, patience and understanding will go a long way in making the most out of the situation.

As you learn more about all the elements of an ecommerce site, you will want to think about who you will hire to build your website. There are so many web-design companies and consultants out there, and the decision can seem overwhelming. A web designer, strictly speaking, creates the look and feel, whereas the web developer or web engineer codes and makes the whole site functional. Website design can cost from one to twenty thousand dollars or more, depending on how many bells and whistles you add. I suggest keeping things simple at first, until you learn more from your analytics data on how your customers interact with your website.

Experience Is Key

Designing a great website is part art and part science, and experience is critical. Above all else, when researching website designers, be sure that they have SEO knowledge. They must know how to build a website that is optimized for search engines, particularly Google. Otherwise, you will end up with a site that costs you more money to market and could be taking a trip far south! In addition, make sure the designer knows how to implement interactive graphical functionality that will not slow down your site. If you choose to ignore this advice, you are buying that ticket to hell right at the start. If you sacrifice this option just to save time or money, you will most likely end up having to rebuild the site altogether.

A key question to ask is whether the codes that your designer implements are proprietary. If so, you should be aware that if you terminate your work relationship with him or her or if you later need the site to be updated by someone else, that portion of the coding may have to be overhauled, which will cost more money. Proprietary coding is not necessarily a bad thing; just be aware of this fact so you are not surprised later on (I learned this lesson the hard way).

When looking for a designer and/or developer, do your homework. Be sure the candidates have a proven ability to build sites that convert (not just a pretty design) and that incorporate industry best practices. Ask for work samples or a portfolio of websites.

- Is the site easy to navigate?
- How does it rank?
- Is the designer flexible and easy to work with?
- Does the developer have good references?
- Is the pricing reasonable - though don't compromise on quality just to get the lowest price?

Web Developer Checklist

☐ Make sure the developer implements clean code.

☐ Find out whether he or she uses proprietary code. Make sure they are willing to give you their source code.

☐ Be sure the developer does not use iFrames for your page design and uses a tableless code.

☐ Make sure the developer uses a combination of HTML and CSS (external CSS code) and uses good CSS techniques.

☐ Limit javascript. Ask the programmer to externalize any javascript files for faster load time and caching. Ask your web developer about asynchronous javascript.

☐ Add fav (favorite) icon. The favicon is a smaller version of your logo that's placed in a browser's location bar.

☐ Check references and portfolios. Make sure he or she has experience building the features and functions you want.

☐ Do not pay the full amount up front; instead, pay a small deposit. Do not pay the final amount until all issues are fixed.

☐ Do not go with the cheapest bid simply because it's the cheapest.

☐ Make sure the developer uses a store platform that is easy to update with content, new products, etc. (Some designers specialize in working with specific store platforms.)

☐ Create a visually appealing and effective 404 error page.

Remember that customer service actually starts when your visitor first clicks on your website. You want your website to have a professional but fluid design that is easy for your visitor to navigate to turn them into customers for your business.

Your Homework

Figure out how you want your website structured and then find developers who can do that. Review in detail competitors' websites as well as websites you like and find easy to use. Interview and hire a designer and/or developer.

Hot Tip: Be sure to host your website on your own hosting account and not that of your designer and/or webmaster. You want full control and access to your website.

Be sure to test your final design on multiple browsers as your site may appear differently on Google Chrome, Safari, Firefox and Internet Explorer.

Section III.

———

The Business of Ecommerce

Chapter 12.

Come Hell or High Water: Promoting Your Store

You will dwell in Ecom Hell if: *you do not learn to love marketing.*

You would probably be surprised at how many web entrepreneurs subscribe to the notion of "Build it and they will come." They think that if their website looks nice, customers will not be able to help but throw money at them. They are sure that come hell or high water, they will succeed because their idea and website are so irresistible. But the real work actually begins when you start promoting your ecommerce store. It is even more difficult for your online store to catch the attention of consumers than an actual physical storefront, so be sure to strategize how you will go about promoting your new business ahead of time.

Marketing an ecommerce store can be done in many ways. As I mentioned briefly earlier, SEO and pay-per-click play major roles in marketing online stores. Other tools include social-media marketing, email marketing, loyalty programs, affiliate marketing, and price-comparison sites, all of which I touch on in this chapter. In short, a passion for advertising (or for learning how to advertise) your business will definitely pay off.

Marketing is also about following up with your customers. Avoid running a website that is merely an order taker. Create and build a relationship with your customers to better understand what their current and long-term needs are. Follow up after each order is placed, especially after the initial order, as this is when you are given the chance to get to know your customers; you have a legitimate reason to call them and introduce yourself. This simple step can help you outshine the competition. Most big companies are not doing this step, because they are simply too big and it is not built into their business process.

Customer Profiles

Create a customer profile. Profiling your customers and their purchases can help you better understand the type of shoppers who come to your website. Some of this information can be gathered when you have the customer on the phone. Keep a list of questions by the customer service phone. Customers who agree to the survey can help you improve your product offering and services to better serve their needs.

Some questions to ask include the following:

- What do you do with our products? Are they for personal use or for gifts?
- How did you come across our website?
- What other sites did you visit before you decided to place your order with us?
- How often would you order this product?
- What kind of products or services do you wish we would carry or have?

Tips for Getting the Most out of Your Customer List

- Focus on adding value. Ensure that your marketing message exudes your core values. Focus on what is in it for the customer. It doesn't matter how great and wonderful your company is; it has to be about the customer.

- Focus on building your brand image. Customer service is marketing, so ensure that all marketing messages and brand proliferation speak positively about your company.
- Seek out testimonials from delighted customers. Capture those testimonials in writing or in video. Ask customers to send in positive reviews through video—you won't get them if you don't ask.
- Make it easy for customers to do business with you. Ensure that all company policies are customer-centric.
- Understand who your customers truly are. Then look for different channels where your customers might be spending their time and money. Go where your customers are; don't wait for them to find you or to search you out.
- Reward your partners and referral sources. Study your analytics, and know where your referral sources are coming from; then contact them to work out an alliance partnership or affiliate arrangement.
- Every lead and every visit is valuable. Always follow through with emails, phone calls, and inquiries, as you never know how one little transaction can lead into bigger contracts or sales in the future.
- Don't ignore your local market. Even though you want to sell nationally, it's easier to optimize your site locally, especially if there is very little competition. This is also a good way to test whether there is potential to create a brick-and-mortar store for your online business.
- Ensure that all your marketing efforts—online, offline, in store, on your blog, on social networks, etc—are coordinated and in sync. Your marketing efforts will be more effective if done in coordination with other campaigns.
- If your products are consumable (e.g., cosmetics, health supplements, food products), be sure to create easy reorder programs. Consider using these products for corporate gifts as well.

If your products are conducive to trial sizes or free samples, be sure to create a sales program in which they can be given away with regular shipments to inform customers of other products on your website.

Search Engine Optimization

As I have said throughout this book, a well-designed site is built first and foremost for the human visitor—the prospective customer. The site should visually and navigationally appeal to the visitor so he or she will be compelled to stay and shop. However, no matter how good your site is, you are going to take a trip to a hot place if customers cannot find it. This is where Internet marketing and search engine optimization (SEO) come into play.

SEO refers to the practice of building and marketing a website in a way that allows visitors to find your site online. Develop an SEO strategy early that you can execute daily, weekly, and monthly to keep ahead of your competition. The key to success with SEO is persistence, tempered with a dose of patience. You need to build enough links without overdoing it. SEO is like an arms race with your competition; you want to do enough to win but not blow your site up. Focus on high-quality sites linking to your site.

SEO is not something you can do and then forget about; rather, SEO is about sustaining campaigns over the long haul. The only way you will see your efforts payoff is through maintaining longevity at the top of search rankings.

Off-page optimization refers to factors outside your own website that lend credibility to your site. These include blogs, forums, directories, and other websites. You can build links to your site by writing articles, doing press releases, and being present in popular social networking sites, such as Facebook and Pinterest. Link building is the process of getting other legitimate sites to link to your site using your specific keywords or your brand to improve your site's search rankings.

On-page optimization refers to the elements on your own website that help search engines recognize your site and understand what your site is about. These elements include a search engine–friendly website structure and well-written copy with appropriate keywords. Add new content to your site each day to keep your site fresh for the search engine bot to crawl. Take the time to really focus on which words and voices your customers respond to in product description; this will help improve your sales conversion, which is a key for long-term success.

No matter who you talk to in the industry, you will hear over and over again that you must have good SEO content for your optimization efforts to work. Good SEO content in ecommerce translates to having excellent product descriptions that help your customers understand how the product you sell will make their lives better and/or solve their problems.

Your content must be grammatically correct, and all words must be spelled correctly. Your content must also connect with your visitor, whether you are describing your product, your company, or your vision. Your visitors are not customers until they buy from you. Your job is to convert them from visitors to customers by making the process as easy as possible so they can find what they are looking for and make that purchase.

Now, search engines like Google and Bing would prefer that you not do "active SEO." They want you to follow best on-page SEO practices, but no off-page SEO. When you engage in optimizing for search engines, do your research and ensure that you proceed with your eyes wide open. Be very careful about overoptimizing your keyword anchor text. The key to success is to have a variety of keywords that are similar in your industry and that denote the same meaning "contextually." Be careful when hiring "SEO experts." If someone promises or guarantees to rank your site at the top of the search engines, you should not walk but run away very quickly.

On-Page Optimization Best Practices

- Use a unique title tag for each page, and make sure it includes significant keywords for that page.
- Include keywords in the domain name.
- Use keywords in alt tag for images.
- Use keywords in meta description,some meta keywords and in surrounding text.
- Use keywords in the site's navigation tools.
- Use keywords in the content body (take into account some keyword density).
- Use keywords in the headings and subheadings within your content.
- Be sure to give keywords prominence in the product description and on the page.

- Use keywords for internal linking.
- Do not use Flash pages, iFrames, or invisible text.
- Do not link to websites without first checking the quality of their links.
- Go wide on your site's link structure instead of deep; nothing should be more than two or three clicks from the home page.
- There should be fewer than one hundred links on each page, especially the home page.
- Make sure your pages are fast loading. Load time plays a big part in SEO.
- Provide new content on your site every day, if possible.
- Keep your site and pages high in terms of theme, as too many categories will dilute your SEO efforts.
- Use synonyms for keywords.
- Do not overuse keywords or stuff them on your pages; you might get an overoptimization penalty.
- Make sure that search engines see what your visitors see on your pages.
- Do not use doorway pages.
- Do not duplicate content from your vendors' sites. Rewrite vendor descriptions to create unique content for your site.
- Use XML sitemaps.

Ask your webmaster to ensure that your website is using canonical uniform resource locators (URLs). This is a difficult concept to explain, but it has to do with ensuring that you don't accidentally have several home pages that actually have the same content. You can read more about this concept at http://www.mattcutts.com/blog/seo-advice-url-canonicalization/.

According to Matt Cutts, Google's head spam catcher, canonicalization is the process of picking the best URL when there are several choices. For example, most people would consider www.example.com, example.com/, www.example.com/index.html, and example.com/home.asp the same. But technically, all of these URLs are different, and a web server could return completely different content for each. When Google "canonicalizes" a URL, it tries to pick the URL that seems like the best representative from that set.

Other On-Page Metrics That Affect SEO

- The amount of time that visitors spend on your site
- The bounce rate—when visitors click off your site without visiting another page
- How often your domain is searched
- Robot.txt files—make sure search engines are crawling your site
- "No follow"—minimize "no follow"; make sure that the links you want followed are followed by search engines
- Clean URL strings with keywords but no session IDs or tracking parameters, which can also become duplicate-content issues

Off-Page Optimization Best Practices

- Use a mixed set of inbound anchor text links.
- Acquire links from old and/or trusted sites.
- A higher prominence of link is better for link value.
- Links from sites with similar or related content are helpful.
- Use one-way inbound links.
- Trickle in link building rather than getting a set number of links each day, week, or month.
- Do not get a site-wide link from another site; this is always a sign that purposeful SEO is in play.
- Do not get linked from a link farm.
- Reciprocal links are not quite dead, but I would not put in a lot of effort to exchange links. Only use reciprocal links when this makes sense. As an example, having reciprocal links with a wedding florist, a wedding photographer, and/or a wedding dress site, as they are in the same industry but not competitors, the link would makes sense.
- Get links from your suppliers and vendors.
- Provide quality content to bloggers, and ask bloggers to review your website or the products you sell. Offer promotions to bloggers if they send traffic to your website.
- Study/audit your competitors' backlinks, and try to gain the same or similar links from the website that is linking to them so long as

you've reviewed their links to be of good quality. Use Majestic SEO tools to study competitors' link quality.

Optimize and build SEO ranking for coupons for your site. Most affiliates rank by optimizing for other brands' coupon codes, so you might as well optimize for your own brand and coupon so that you can garner the extra free traffic without having to share the revenue or pay an affiliate commission.

Press Releases for SEO

Traditionally, a press release was a marketing piece written and distributed by a company to communicate news and announcements to the press. Today, it is still a great purpose that can now be coupled with a way to publish news so that search engines and prospective customers will find your site on the Internet.

Press releases are generally written in an objective voice, without editorializing. Just about any topic can be the subject of a press release, but it should be newsworthy, not blatant advertising, and should definitely include your anchor text links and contact information. Other than that, the basic principles of the traditional press release are still valid: a good, newsworthy topic; grammatically correct content; third-person point of view; and factual content that is to the point.

"But I'm Not Running a Big Company. Do I Really Need Press Releases?"

Let's be clear: If you are in the ecommerce industry and you rely on search engine results to attract customers, the answer is *yes*! You will get much more bang for your buck if you include press releases in your SEO marketing mix.

Unlike a traditional press release, the SEO press release contains new elements like embedded hyperlinks to your site, which instantly make the release interactive. When an SEO press release is submitted to public relations websites, it is picked up by Google, Yahoo! News, and many other outlets. Including keyword links that describe your business (a.k.a. anchor text) helps to send relevant traffic to your site, because anchor text is used in the algorithms to determine a page's ranking.

A search engine's primary job is to produce quality content for web surfers. When someone searches Google for "oil-free suntan lotion," Google tries to produce as much quality content about that topic as their search engines can find. Regularly creating and submitting press releases that include anchor text (your keywords) will increase your site's visibility in the organic search results. These are the links that are not sponsored or paid-for ads.

On-Page and Off-Page SEO for Press Releases

As mentioned earlier, on-page optimization is what you do to your own website (in product descriptions, photos, web-page titles, keyword tags, etc) to make it keyword relevant. When published on your company's website, a press release is new keyword-rich content that search engines can crawl and index.

Off-page SEO using a press release is achieved when you publish a press release that is linked through third-party sites. The higher the third-party site ranks, the better off you will be. Search rankings are like popularity contests—the more popular your associates are, the more popular you are. Links to your website from third-party press-release distribution sites and blogs (off-page SEO) also create what's called *backlinks* to your site. Backlinks are another way to reinforce your rank in the popularity contest known as page rank.

Other elements of the new press release include video, photos, other multimedia, and social media tags (RSS feeds, social-networking or bookmarking links) that help search engines label your site as useful content so they appear when queries are run on your target keywords.

Social media tags also allow readers to share information with their networks, thus acting like advertisers for your business. Remember that from an SEO perspective, regularly issuing press releases, even during months when nothing seems newsworthy, is beneficial. If you are pressed for ideas, consider all of your business's audiences: the media, customers, vendors, current and prospective employees, investors, and industry analysts, to name a few. Write a few different press releases for each segment. The following list should help you come up with ideas for when to write a press release.

Types of Press Releases

- Affiliate programs
- Awards and honors
- Book publication (contributions and published works)
- Call for papers
- Case studies
- Cause marketing (charity, donations)
- Crisis communication
- Corporate restructuring
- Discontinued products
- Events
- Expert commentary (trends, contrarian viewpoint)
- Financial news
- Grant awards
- Holidays
- Industry trends
- Job fair
- Mergers and acquisitions
- New company launch
- New design wins or joint marketing
- New geographic market opening
- New hire (senior level)
- New product launch
- New software and updates
- New store opening
- New webcast, podcast, or video
- New website launch
- New vertical market
- Product recall
- Public company listing

- Public service announcements
- Publications (articles, research journals, etc)
- Request for proposals
- Restaurant review
- Retirement (senior level)
- Sales and discount codes
- Seasonal topics and promotional items (New Year's, Valentine's Day, St. Patrick's Day, Mother's Day, etc)
- Seminars or webinars (educational events)
- Speaking engagements
- Store closures or liquidation
- Surveys, studies, and poll results (and related company information, including epidemiological data)
- Tradeshows

Press Release Dos

- Do keyword research instead of randomly selecting your anchor text.
- Use good grammar, and keep the length between four and six hundred words.
- Include one or more quotes from subject-matter experts.
- Include up to three keyword-rich anchor text links, with the main keywords appearing within the first sixty-five characters of the release.
- Use long-tail keywords.
- Write for human readers first and then for search engines.

Press Release Don'ts

- Don't stuff keywords into the headline; the headline should flow naturally.
- Don't use "click here" or "more information" links. Instead, be descriptive with your links. Use a keyword anchor text that can be use to link back to your website. But keep it natural.

- Don't use the words *you*, *yours*, *our(s)*, *we*, except in quotes.
- Don't put off submitting press releases. Schedule your press releases and content for the entire year (you can always make last-minute changes to this schedule on the fly).
- Don't change anchor text to different keywords each month. Maintain one or two consistent keywords to achieve page rank. Introduce a new keyword once you achieve results for the first two.

Chapter 13.

Social Networks

You will go to Ecom Hell if: *you run an introverted website.*

Social networks, such as Facebook and Twitter, have single-handedly changed marketing as we know it. Millions of people are using social media to keep in touch with friends, to date, to choose restaurants, or to conduct product research. Why are marketers so aflutter with excitement about social media? For marketers, understanding consumer preferences and behavior is fundamental to the job, and these social networks, with their tell-all profiles, are rich sources of consumer information.

Because of the connectedness, a social network can exponentially amplify word-of-mouth advertising. In addition, more than ever before, with Google shopping no longer free and the increasing costs in pay-per-click, having as many means as possible to keep connected to your fans and customer base is crucial.

The advent of social media levels the marketing playing field, so that even small businesses can achieve results that their big-box competitors would envy, but without the big budget.

Facebook

Facebook connects people and has become a powerful marketing tool that creates a bridge between customers and businesses. However, many marketers fail to maximize the use of Facebook for ecommerce by inadvertently committing mistakes that hurt their marketing efforts. Facebook can help drive traffic to your ecommerce site and provide leads. Incorporate Facebook into your marketing strategy as a cost-effective way of connecting with customers, old and new alike, wherever they are.

Before anything else, determine whether your Facebook page is going to be a group page or a fan page. Groups allow interaction on a smaller scale, whereas fan pages can have an unlimited number of fans—even beyond the five-thousand-friend limit. For businesses, fan pages are ideal. But targeting Facebook users does not stop with creating a fan page and collecting lots of fans.

Facebook Checklist

☐ Create a strategy. Know how to connect with Facebook's massive audience in a significant way. Take time to consider a few things:

- Who are you targeting?
- How can you invite fans?
- What is your message?

Not having a clear social media strategy is a big mistake. Do not assume that once you have built your page, people will come and "like" it. You still need to plan when to post updates, which news or links to share, where to promote the page, how to deal with customer service issues that are aired publicly by customers on your Facebook page, and so on.

☐ Avoid focusing on the number of fans. Focus instead on engaging your fan base. Users "like" pages that are appealing and active. Share relevant news and articles that will engage your fans. Add content that is useful and interesting. Share valuable tips.

☐ Be active on your page. Having a fan page with no admin activity is worse than not having a page at all. Take note: People can "unlike" your page as quickly as they liked it. Aside from posting regularly, show fans that you are listening by monitoring their page activities and responding to their queries and comments. Pay attention to what your fans are interested in, even if the topic is not related to what you do. To be interesting, you have to be interested first.

☐ Customer relations matter: Be sure to have a customer support workflow built into your Facebook social strategy. Be mindful that customers will not hesitate to air disputes publicly on Facebook. Therefore, you will need to be extra vigilant about monitoring what's being said about your brand and about addressing customer service issues promptly and attentively.

☐ Let your customers get to know you. Share company photos or information on interesting individuals and employees with your fans. The key is to make a connection with your customers.

☐ Create interesting surveys and polls. Ask your fans to participate in your marketing efforts.

☐ Always know what your competitors are up to on their Facebook pages.

☐ Try different engagement campaigns, like contests, that resonate with your customers.

☐ Be focused and get your message across, but don't dwell and linger. Time spent on Facebook can get out of hand. Be mindful that you're not wasting valuable time that can be allocated on other actionable tasks for your business.

☐ Add value. Do not make this all about selling. Ninety percent of the time adding value and 10 percent of the time selling is a good formula to follow if you are unsure on what would be a safe number to start off with.

☐ Use your fan pages or groups as your focus groups. Get your customers to vote on what products you should be developing, designing, or selling.

☐ Look into "interest lists" for Facebook. It may work for your business if you can create niche interest topics that your customers might really be "interested" in. For example, I might create a list that covers "celebrity weddings."

☐ Facebook ads can be successful if your offer is very targeted and unbeatable. We once ran a product sale that was too good to pass up; based on that experience and subsequent ad campaigns, we learned that a very targeted offer works.

Twitter

With seventy-five million users, Twitter can help extend a marketer's reach and drive traffic to ecommerce sites. However, many ecommerce storeowners are still wary of using Twitter as part of their marketing efforts, thinking that tweeting regularly requires too much work. In addition, some have a concern about revealing too much company information.

Fortunately, the benefits of Twitter for your business outweigh the downsides. Done right, tweeting can help you promote your business, connect with customers, and give your brand a personality. Building a solid Twitter following can also help drive traffic to your site. Twitter, like Facebook, has social signals that can indeed influence your website ranking on the search engines.

Building an active Twitter account with many followers will take some time and effort—and even money if you are paying someone to maintain your Twitter account. But it is worthwhile.

Twitter Checklist

☐ Have a plan.

- What is your objective for using Twitter?
- Is it for marketing or branding purposes?
- Are you going to post product details and offers?
- Or is it exclusively for receiving and providing feedback?

If you don't have a strategic Twitter plan, let your main objective (marketing or branding) be the focus of your tweets.

☐ Be open, but not too much. It's okay to tweet about your business life, as this helps you to create a connection with your followers. But do not deviate too much from your focus. If you want to give blow-by-blow details of your personal life, open a personal account.

☐ Whatever you do, always reply to a direct message. Do not underestimate the power of tweets. One negative tweet from an unhappy customer could cost your business its reputation. Protect your brand by addressing complaints promptly. Your business Twitter account is as important as your customer service department.

☐ Allot at least fifteen minutes a day for tweeting. Keep your account active, and engage followers by tweeting regularly, whether it's replying to other tweets, scheduling tweets, or following new followers. Try using a mobile Twitter app on your cell phone to keep up.

☐ Stay focused and be strategic. To stay on task, comment only on topics related to your business or that may interest your customers. Comment when you have something useful to add. Become a thought leader in your field, and you will steadily earn more followers.

Pinterest Marketing

One of the fastest-growing social sites is Pinterest. In the world of social media, it's a fairly new site. However, Pinterest has already proven itself to be an effective tool for driving traffic to ecommerce retailers. Shareaholic's "Referral Traffic Report" noted that Pinterest generated more referrals than Google+ and YouTube combined. In fact, Pinterest already boasts nearly ten million active users—up from just under two million in early 2011. Those are some pretty impressive stats. Maybe there is something to this Pinterest thing after all.

Pinterest is a visual social media site. Customers, or potential customers, can only pin pictures and videos of your product (not text). So make sure that your product images are not loaded with rich media that cannot be found by Pinterest. The best way to use Pinterest is to make pinning your product as easy as possible for participants. Include a "PinIt" link next to your product images, whether those images are on your website, blog, or other social sources. (Most retailers tend to put the link next to either the product description or the price to make this convenient.) You can split test pages with and without prices to see which version converts better. Using the "PinIt" bookmark to add items to your board can boost your content, which also makes your board more appealing.

Unlike other marketing efforts, Pinterest can grow your business for free. Talk about a bargain in today's streamlined business world! Pinterest enables you to target your customers, more so than social media giants Facebook and Twitter. Traffic to your Facebook page, for example, mostly comes from people who are interested in your business, but not necessarily in a particular product. Traffic to your Pinterest board, on the other hand, comes from people who are interested in a product. Just like Facebook users can "like" something and share it with others, Pinterest users can "pin" something and "repin" (or share) it with others. Most users who "pin" something are doing so on purpose; you are not likely to get many people pinning your stuff by accident, which means it is easier to target your customer base. When an item you are selling on your website is pinned by a Pinterest user, it can help grow your business, because the visual pin also functions as a direct link to your product page. This means more traffic for you.

People who use Pinterest tend to focus more on products than on brands. Somebody may pin one product from your website and another from your competitor's website and then purchase the one that is cheaper. This is why you want to establish your brand on Pinterest. When you create your Pinterest account, don't just pin products from your website, as this shows that you're only promoting yourself. Instead, include a mix of products from various sources to make your board a gathering spot for people interested in the products listed on your board. This will give you a better shot at generating more conversions.

When you sign up for a Pinterest account, you are assigned a unique URL (e.g., pinterest.com/yourdomainname). This means you can use Google Analytics to track pins and other details. This, in turn, lets you know which items are popular and where you should put your focus when looking to generate more conversions. You'll also be able to track referral traffic to see where your "pins" are coming from. With careful monitoring and minor adjustments based on the stats you receive, Pinterest can be a valuable marketing tool.

Another benefit to having a Pinterest board is that Pinterest is starting to rank on the organic search results. To learn more about Pinterest, read *Pinterest Marketing: An Hour a Day* by Jennifer Evans Cario.

Social Bookmarking

Like the term implies, social bookmarking is, above all, social. This is a means for people to categorize and share their favorite links with others. Social bookmarks give consumers a way to access their bookmarks from any computer, as they are not stored in one machine but on the web (just like your Yahoo! or Gmail email boxes). By adding keyword tags, the social bookmarks provide a public forum for consolidating disparate web content into groups of similar data. The ability to add keyword tags helps SEO, and the sharing of links virally can help expose your brand to new audiences. Add social bookmarking tags to your pages to enable customers to share pages and products they find useful.

Top Social Bookmarking Sites

- AllMyFaves
- BLiNK
- Blogmarks
- Delicious
- Digg

- Driigo
- Reddit
- Slashdot
- StumbleUpon
- TweetMeme

Blogs

Several times, I have mentioned the idea of becoming a thought leader. You might be wondering just how one achieves that status or level of confidence. The blog, shortened from the term *web log*, is a forum for posting online journal entries. Blogs have catapulted many bloggers to semi-celebrity status within their respective niche markets. Good blogs become public forums for sharing common interests, knowledge, and other useful (or even useless) information.

In the early days, blogging was thought to be merely a hobbyist's pursuit. But early adopters could see the makings of a new media form emerging. Today, bloggers have become self-proclaimed experts, with the power to draw millions of followers who keep up with their every post through RSS feeds, social networks, and email subscriptions. TechCrunch, a popular start-up news blog, and the Huffington Post are two examples of successful media outlets that began as blogs.

Blogs allow ordinary people to become thought leaders in their chosen areas. But how is the consumer protected from being hoodwinked by opportunistic posers? The beauty of this system is that the public collectively decides whether a blogger is legitimate or a fraud. And believe me, they will identify and publicly oust fakes. Just like the market, with its ability to separate the wheat from the chaff, the public puts bloggers to intense scrutiny. So a word of caution: If you plan to blog, be sure to choose a topic that you are knowledgeable and capable of writing about. If not, be prepared to do a lot of research.

Setting up a blog is fairly simple, and many ecommerce platforms include a blog option. CMS's (content management systems), such as Wordpress, have customizable templates that make setting up a blog easier; they also accommodate mobile blogging for those on the go. Your blog can be part of your website (yourdomain.com/blog) or a standalone entity (yourblog.com). Adding social networking tags will allow readers to share posts they like or find useful.

Reasons to Blog

- Forum for sharing your expertise
- Search engine optimization (keyword-rich content that you can link to your ecommerce site)
- Engage customers and provide valuable information on your products
- Allows control over content regarding your product
- Gain feedback from customers
- Create a following for your brand (branding)
- Provide another customer touch point for your product
- Help guide customer decision making

Social Media Strategy Tips

- Set clear goals that you want to achieve with your social media campaign—for example, create brand awareness, increase sales, and so on.
- Create a strategy to achieve your social media goals—for example, sponsor a contest where the winner will receive your products and then share and promote the contest on Twitter and Facebook.
- Develop tactical steps for implementing strategy—for example, monitoring, responding, posting, community building, and so on. Social media is not a passive project; it's an ongoing activity to create a connection with your potential and past customer base.
- Do not be overtly "salesy." Make sure that you focus on providing value, engaging your fans, and being interesting (as well as being interested in what your fans are interested in).
- Be consistent in your frequency and voice when adding content to social media.

Chapter 14.

Email Marketing

You will agonize in Ecom Hell if: *you do not continually engage with your customers.*

Email marketing is still the undisputed cheapest way to connect and sell directly to your existing and past customer base. There is no doubt among marketers that this method is highly effective, despite the increasing usage of smart phones. There is also no dispute that planning email campaigns, creating promotions, and maintaining a viable customer list requires knowledge and work.

Email marketing is inexpensive compared with other forms of advertising and is an easy way to track results with an embedded links feature to your site.

To begin, you need a list of email addresses (database) and a system to create and send emails. Web-based email marketing solutions or "autoresponders" include AWeber, Constant Contact, MailChimp, Infusionsoft, and VerticalResponse.

Use email marketing to reach out to past customers, offer special deals to current customers, or just let more customers know about your brand, products, and services. But whatever you do, *don't* purchase a list of email addresses. Purchasing lists can be expensive, they rarely work, and they could put you in a position of violating spam laws. If these customers complain (and they will), your ISP or email marketing tool may blacklist you from sending future emails.

Create compelling emails that will entice your recipient to open your email message. Most inboxes are a nightmare to begin with, and sifting through all the emails can be a daunting task for anyone. That is why your email needs to grab your customers' attention with either an attractive subject line or a promotional offer or both. It's also important to address the recipient by his or her first name, as that will make your customer more likely to open the email.

One of the more frequent questions I am asked is how often companies should send emails. This really depends on your company and the type of business you're in. What you don't want is for your customers to experience "email fatigue," for which the only remedy is to unsubscribe from your list.

Instead, you need to segment your list to reduce the likelihood that recipients will unsubscribe. Some ways to segment your list are to group the list by the last time the customer was active, by what the customer purchased, or by the category of product that he or she purchased. By segmenting your list, your email marketing efforts can be more targeted and therefore more relevant to your customer.

Other types of emails can run on autopilot once they are properly set up. For example, a drip campaign offers a series of strategic product promotions relevant to your customers. Other autopilot emails include order confirmation, shipment confirmation, and abandoned cart emails, which can all be automatically triggered when a set of actions takes place. These autopilot emails should work behind the scenes, so you do not have to worry about them on a daily basis. However, you should review them periodically to ensure that they are still relevant and up-to-date.

Other occasions to email customers include new product additions to your website, sales, birthday/anniversary gifts, or other promotions. You can opt to send an email for a single promotion or in a newsletter format to cover multiple topics on a regular basis. Whether you send a newsletter monthly, bimonthly, or quarterly, make sure to keep your look and message consistent.

Whether you are doing your email marketing campaign yourself or hiring someone, be sure to measure your ROI. Those late-night hours you spend crafting emails and managing the program should be rewarded.

Email Campaigns

Here are some additional tips for a successful email marketing campaign:

Give Customers a Reason to Sign Up

Enter customers who sign up in a contest for a shopping spree on your site. Ask customers to submit photos or videos of your products in their home, and then award prizes for innovative product use through your email newsletter. Allow customers to share their experiences with your products and services (product reviews) and involve them in discussions.

Use Catchy but Relevant Subject Lines

Consumers have become so desensitized by huge discounts that a subject line boasting 10 percent off may not be enough to get your email opened. Remember that your audience has very little time to read all of the emails they sign up for, so make sure your compelling offer stands out from the onslaught. Promotional emails typically have one day to get your customers' attention. After that, the chances of someone going back and opening the email diminish greatly, so you must have an eye-catching, attention-grabbing subject line. If possible, make your message so enticing that in addition to opening the email, people go out of their way to forward and post it on blogs and other forums.

Provide Both HTML and Text Formats

Some readers dislike emails that contain a lot of images, especially on mobile devices. It's debatable which is more successful at conversion—text-only or HTML emails that include images. Each audience is different, and you should test your customers' likes and dislikes. Try both types by using the A/B testing feature offered by some web-based email providers to see which gets higher open and click-through rates. Alternatively, you can send both HTML and text versions (many email systems allow both). With so many people now opening their emails via their smart phones and tablets, you want to ensure that your emails will render properly. Be sure to look into responsive email design to ensure that your email gets opened.

Newsletter-Style Emails

You might be tempted to send out email blasts frequently with promotions. *Don't!* At least one email a month should be in the format of a tip or advice (remember, you are a thought leader). Keep the same guidelines as you would for sending personal emails to friends and family: make the message relevant and not junk. Use this format to connect and engage with your readers and provide value for them so they will stay on your list. Subscribers want quality, useful information. They do not want to be inundated constantly with in-your-face advertising and promotions.

Test and Optimize Landing Pages

For most email campaigns, a reader should be directed to a special campaign landing page on your website, instead of just linking to your home page. A landing page is the page on your website dedicated to providing more information about a promotion. With a well-written landing page, you can keep your emails short and to the point. Make sure your landing pages and emails match, from look and feel to language and tone. They do not have to be identical, but the messaging should be aligned. Remember to optimize for mobile and tablet viewing as well.

Additional Email Campaign Tips

Once you have mastered the basics, there are some additional marketing elements you may want to incorporate into your email campaigns. Social media, trigger campaigns, drip campaigns, segmentation, embedding product videos into emails, re-targeting ads and personalization are some examples you can try. The key is to start today. Learn from your buyers' behavior to see which email campaigns they respond to. Ensure that your campaigns are integrated with your overall marketing and growth strategies instead of using the occasional hit-and-run tactics. Every time you email your customers for whatever reason, even when it's just to acknowledge that you received a returned item, you have the opportunity to reconnect and reengage. This will lead them back to your site. Be creative; your emails do not have to be run-of-the-mill with boring, template verbiage. Never waste the golden opportunity to connect with your customers.

I still remember with fondness a successful email series that we executed really well. It started with a compelling offer: $5.00 bridesmaid tote bags. In each email after that, we noted the quantity of bags already sold on the emails' "hero shot" (the main image). This created a sense of urgency and popularity. The deal was so good that customers were posting the offer onto online forums and talking about it among their communities.

Types of Email Campaigns

- Drip (or series) campaigns—a series of emails that you roll out, usually done automatically
- Newsletter—about your company, new products, your customers as a community
- New product announcements
- Order confirmation
- Shipment confirmation
- Abandoned cart emails—follow up (preferably with coupons) to bring the customer back to make a final purchase
- Promotions and sales
- Product in-stock notification
- Order refunded
- Returned merchandise received

Finally, one of the most important emails, which you need to send promptly is the order confirmation email. Immediately after a customer checks out, send a follow-up email thanking the customer for the purchase, along with a receipt or billing status, order status, and tracking and shipping info, if available. Providing this information is an ecommerce best practice that customers have come to expect. It also reduces the volume of "where's my order?" calls, which can tie up your customer service department.

Email Best Practices Checklist

☐ Personalize your emails.

☐ Fine-tune your subject line. Be sure it is catchy and attention getting, as this will affect the open rate.

☐ Create compelling content with a clear call to action by focusing on offers and expiration dates to create urgency.

☐ Don't send only promotional emails. Be sure to send emails on topics that are interesting to your demographic/customer base as well. You want to be the thought leader in your industry, so you need to help educate your customer. For example, if you sell kitchen products, send out new recipes or cooking techniques related to your product.

☐ Schedule your email campaigns. Create email calendars, and keep track of past promotions and offers. Be consistent; establish a pattern that your customers can count on.

☐ Use Google Analytics in conjunction with email tools to track metrics of every email campaign (e.g., the open rate, number of emails sent, conversion rate, sales revenue, etc).

☐ Send out emails on holidays.

☐ Make your offer/promotion too good to pass up. Make it irresistible.

☐ Highlight your promotion clearly. Ensure that your customer understands the value of your offer.

☐ Send both HTML and text-only emails.

☐ Test links inside every email before sending to make sure they take readers to the proper page. In addition, make sure the images are linked correctly and coded for alt tags.

☐ Segment your lists. For example, allow customers to choose which types of emails they want to receive, or send emails based on customers' historical purchases.

☐ Make it easy to unsubscribe from your email list. If you segment the types of emails you send, this does not have to be a complete opt-out. (For example, give them the option of receiving once-a-week emails rather than daily. Or allow them to receive one type of email but not another.)

☐ Add social widgets, such as Facebook and Twitter links, to enable easy sharing.

☐ Test your email through a spam filter before sending.

☐ Incorporate video into your emails. These can be very simple, such as a quick video on a newly launched product.

☐ Ensure that all marketing campaigns are consistently promoted on all channels, including Facebook, Twitter, your website, etc.

☐ Inform your affiliates when you are running promotions so they can also market them to their lists.

☐ Entice visitors to opt-in with single-use coupons.

☐ Auto opt-in at checkout. Some customers may complain, but most won't mind. Just be sure to make unsubscribing to your email list painless.

☐ Test different days of the week. Optimize offers on the days that are slowest for your business. (Wednesdays are typically slow days.)

☐ When running a promotion, run a series campaign to gently remind your customers throughout the length of the promotion:

- Notify customers of the upcoming sale promotion.
- Notify customers that the end of the promotion is approaching (e.g., in the next two days).
- Notify customers of the last day of the promotion.

☐ Provide your full company information on all emails, so recipients know who is responsible.

☐ Don't buy email lists, don't sell your list, and don't spam your customers.

Email Marketing Metrics:

- Open rate – How many emails were opened by receipient?
- Bounce rate = How many emails were rejected? Meaning these email addresses are no longer valid.
- Deliver rate – How many emails were received that is on your list?
- Click Thru rate – How many opened the email and clicked the offer or promotion?
- Conversion rate – How many made a purchase?
- Unsubscribe rate – How many wanted to be off your email list and longer want to receive emails from your company?

Chapter 15.

Affiliate Programs

Affiliates are like the Elves and the Shoemaker. You wake up in the morning and there is more money in your bank account.

—Zen Zamayr

You will undergo Ecom Hell if: *you ignore the power of affiliates.*

An affiliate marketing program involves individuals or businesses who act like a sales force for your products. You pay an advertiser to target only the prospects that fit your niche, and you only pay them for results.

You can recruit potential affiliates yourself or through third-party affiliate networks. If you want to do the research yourself, sign up with affiliate communities (search Google using your keywords to find these communities) or sign up where your competitors are. The reason you want to partner with an affiliate that your competitors are also using is that the affiliate is already marketing to the demographic interested in what you are selling. The affiliates are already selling your competitors' products; you just have to make your partnership with them more relevant and fruitful for them so they promote your site more.

Third-party affiliate networks, such as ClickBank, LinkShare, ShareASale, AvantLink, and Commission Junction, give you access to hundreds of relevant affiliates. In return, you share a percentage with them (usually 10 percent of the commission paid to the affiliate). For example, if you paid one hundred dollars in commissions to your affiliate, you would pay the third-party affiliate network a ten dollar fee for connecting you to that affiliate, the total cost to you is one hundred and ten dollars. You can certainly try to do all this on your own with software available, but I have found that using the third-party affiliate service is much easier. These services pay commissions, and many give you access to their network of affiliate partners.

The secret to a successful affiliate marketing program is in the relationships you develop. Remember, affiliates are conduits to your niche (they are not your competition), so make the relationship a priority and help them reach their goals. Let them know in advance of your promotional schedule, provide tools, such as ad creative (e.g., artwork, banners, product photos), and send any new and exclusive content, if possible. Reward super affiliates with better commissions, exclusive products, and promotions. Once a good working relationship is established, you may ask affiliates to email their audience on your behalf.

With the ever-changing state laws on sales tax, be sure to check with your state government on requirements for collecting sales tax on affiliate partner sales leads. You should also check with local municipalities and the county where your business is located. Complicated sales tax laws can cause lots of confusion, and if you are not careful, you may be charged interest and penalty fees during a sales tax audit.

Affiliate Checklist

☐ Provide banner graphics that advertise your product and other creative copy to affiliates.

☐ Inform affiliate partners ahead of time of your promotional calendar.

☐ Reward super affiliates with higher commissions and exclusive deals. In return, they will usually promote your site to a higher position on their website (higher visibility or placement).

☐ Sponsor some of your affiliates' email blasts.

☐ Inform affiliates when you have new products.

☐ Provide affiliates with product videos and how-tos.

☐ Sponsor contests or shopping sprees for affiliates.

☐ Pay all commissions on time. (An affiliate service does this for you.)

☐ Focus on your top 20 percent affiliates (the ones that bring you 80 percent of your affiliate sales revenue).

☐ Track and measure affiliate performance and work with them to better promote your site and your affiliate's site.

☐ Rewrite the product descriptions that you give your affiliates. You want to avoid duplicate content. If your affiliate's site has been around longer than yours, it is likely to show up for the keywords that you are trying to rank for. In addition, your site might get hit with a duplicate content penalty.

☐ Have an agreement about when and how your affiliate may be permitted to use PPC to advertise your brand.

☐ Monitor refund rates on affiliate sales. Ensure that the refund rate is not abnormal in comparison with your normal return rate (usually under 4 percent). This is because in addition to issuing refunds, you have also already paid a commission on that sale that you ultimately do not get back.

☐ Watch out for duplicate payments to multiple affiliate partners for the same transaction. Ensure that the cookie that is recognized by your affiliate program is the last one (the last affiliate cookie gets credit for the sale).

☐ Attend affiliate conferences, such as the Affiliate Summit, to get to know the players in the industry.

Comparison-Shopping Engines

In a grocery aisle, one of the first things a customer typically does is look at the price tag and compare the price with other brands. This practice is the basic idea behind comparison-shopping engines, which allow shoppers to review product information and compare related elements, such as product ratings, customer reviews, and, most important, the product's price. Shoppers are given the option to search according to category or keyword, both of which bring up a list of products from different retailers.

As a retailer, you are encouraged to send comparison-shopping engines your product names or titles, images, descriptions, price information, and other important product-related details. All of this information is sent as a "product feed," which is then uploaded to the comparison-shopping engine site.

Most consumers browse price-comparison sites right before making a decision, which makes it a great opportunity to increase your conversion rate. In general, shoppers have already researched the items they are looking for, so they are there just to make a final decision about where to buy a product they have already decided on.

Customers are likely to choose the first products they see listed on comparison sites. Assuming you have done your homework and made your items look better (or lower-priced) than others' on the list, shoppers will not have to compare much. By showcasing your product next to other premium products in its category, your listing increases your brand's image. In addition, when used as a standard for comparison, your product becomes top of mind among shoppers.

A general misconception is that investing in comparison-shopping engines is a huge risk and an unnecessary expense. This may be because some comparison sites offer a cost-per-click model, which means you pay an "advertising" fee each time someone clicks on your product. But what you should take advantage of at first are the lower-cost services. Google Product Search, for example, is the largest among the lower-cost display shopping sites. (It used to be free.) In fact, according to a recent survey, Google Product Search is the biggest revenue driver for online retailers, closely followed by Nextag (a service that also offers paid placement and sponsored listings). As you get the hang of the process (or finally have the budget), you may want to try the cost-per-click model offered by sites, such as Shopping.com, PriceGrabber.com, and myTriggers.com, where you basically compete on price. Check out YourStoreWizards.com for product feed services.

After you get listed on these comparison-shopping engines, prepare your inventory in anticipation of your success. Many retailers get blindsided by the sudden surges in traffic and sales as a result of their listings. As a failsafe, always check your inventory and make sure not to list products that are in short supply.

As with any marketing program, you will want to ensure that the dollars spent are working for your business. Regularly measuring a program's ROI will help you decide which programs work and which you may want to discontinue. As always, be prudent, maintain your profit margins, and stop bleeding money by measuring ROI.

Personally, I have never had much luck with the paid-for comparison engines; I have only seen my account drained quickly without any ROI. However, I do believe that comparison engines work well for things like electronic products, where people search a specific make and model. For general goods, on the other hand, it may be harder to turn a profit. But do not get discouraged. Try out new ideas and different methods even if you have a small budget; it is worth learning if a channel is right for your business.

Your Homework

1. Sign up for an email account.
2. Create all social media accounts for your site: Facebook, Twitter, LinkedIn, Pinterest, etc.
3. Sign up with an affiliate network.
4. Upload photos and product descriptions on the affiliate website or give them to a designer who can help you.
5. Add product details into your back end.

6. Create a shipping chart or shipping rules.
7. Sign up with shipping vendors like UPS and FedEx. Sign up for shipping software that does rate comparison if you already know what you want/need (but wait until you have some history before taking this step).

Chapter 16.

Pay-per-Click and Keywords

Pay-per-Click Advertising

Pay-per-click (PPC) is an online advertising method in which you only pay when a visitor clicks on your ad link. As part of the PPC campaign, you choose which keywords your ad will target and what rank your ad will have when someone searches for related keywords. The amount you pay is directly proportional to the competitiveness of the keywords you choose, so that's where long-tail keywords will help both with the cost of your campaign and the likelihood of conversion.

During the time our site was absent from Google, I learned how to use Google AdWords to bring traffic to our site and also dabbled a bit with Yahoo! and Bing. Mostly, we focused on Google AdWords, because we got most of our traffic from Google. AdWords helped us learn which keywords were converting and which products were selling because of those keywords. During the initial learning phase, we lost money on our campaigns, but over time, as we fine-tuned our keywords and tested ad copy, we started garnering positive ROI (up to 600 percent and conversion rates as high as 3.5 percent). In the end, Google AdWords enabled us to stay in business while we waited for our SEO ranking to return. After that experience, we continued to rely on PPC to grow the ecommerce store, especially with the launch of new estores.

When you first set up your AdWords account, make sure that you set up the correct time zone. I made this mistake once on one account and didn't realize it until we ran way too many campaigns. (To learn more about Google AdWords, check out *Advanced Google AdWords* by Brad Geddes.) Running a pay-per-click campaign can be a challenging but rewarding task. It's exhilarating to see your ad campaigns converting into sales on the one hand; on the other hand, however, this can be a hair-pulling experience. I experienced both extremes while managing my own website's PPC campaigns.

Follow some of these best practices for managing PPC campaigns, and you will start driving targeted traffic to your website.

Google PPC Checklist

☐ Set a daily budget, increasing it incrementally as you experience better ROI and conversion success. After all, why limit how many sales your site can generate (unless there's a supply issue)?

☐ Pause unprofitable keywords (keywords that get lots of impressions but no clicks or don't convert).

☐ Test day-parting tool. Study which times people are shopping on your site and adjust accordingly.

☐ Run smaller groups of keyword buckets (small groups of similar keywords).

☐ Run exact-match and phrase-match campaigns. If you only use broad match, you can burn through your ad budget pretty quickly.

☐ When you run the exact-match and phrase-match campaigns, set your bid a bit higher than what you would pay for a broad-match campaign.

You will need to test this to determine if this strategy makes sense for your ad group.

☐ Bid as much as you are willing to pay to acquire a customer versus what you're hoping to pay. Sometimes people underbid, which actually costs them the quality traffic that they want.

☐ Run a manageable keyword list until you have a proven track record of positive ROI. (In other words, don't have too large a keyword list.)

☐ Focus on optimizing your ad groups not just keywords alone.

☐ Set up a negative keyword bucket list.

☐ Pay attention to the click-through rate.

☐ Set up Google Analytics to capture sales transaction data. If you don't, you won't know your money keyword value.

☐ Test images for AdWords.

☐ Turn off content network, unless you know that this is a cheap and profitable way to acquire new traffic.

☐ Know what your product margins and breakeven point are. This is especially important in determining the highest bid you're willing to pay to acquire a customer. If there is longer lifetime value potential, it may be worth paying a little more up front, as long as you have the back end to support future revenue creation. The goal is to amortize your acquisition cost.

☐ Always be testing your ad copy. Use different versions of your ad copy that you can test against. Once you have a proven model, constantly test against the winner.

☐ Study your competitors' ad copy and landing pages.

☐ Try competitor spying tools like Ispionage.com.

☐ Focus on improving your conversion rate. The goal is to maximize your visitor value (converting to a sale) rather than only increase the amount of traffic.

☐ Review your Google Analytics data consistently. Take fifteen to twenty minutes a day to review your key performance indicators (KPIs) and the key data points that are actionable. This will also help you determine which keywords are important to your site, as well as which keywords are your money keywords.

☐ Focus on improving your "quality score" for your ad campaigns. If your ad has a quality score that Google likes, it will show up higher (in terms of placement), and you will pay less for your ad in comparison to your competitors. In effect, Google is rewarding you for your higher CTR. It may even move your ad to the number-one placement but only charge you the number-two placement rate. It's a win-win situation for you and Google.

☐ Pay attention to your keyword money terms. Your goal is to convert highest for your money keywords.

☐ Use dynamic keyword insertion, which automatically inserts your keyword into your ad copy. Done correctly, this can help you boost your CTR.

☐ Ensure that the landing page for your ad copy is relevant to what the searcher selected. In addition, make sure your ad copy message stays consistent. If you offer free shipping, make sure your landing page has the same message.

☐ Do not operate your PPC on autopilot. You can be sure that your competitors, who are also paying for traffic, are watching their campaigns like a hawk. Keeping a close eye on your PPC will make all the difference in whether your company is profitable.

Chapter 17.

Operating Your Business

You will slide into Ecom Hell if: *you hate routine work and documenting your workflow.*

Profit in business comes from repeat customers, customers that boast about your product or service, and that bring friends with them.

—W. Edwards Deming

I'm really excited to get to the topic of operating your business. Many entrepreneurs focus all their efforts on getting the sale, rather than on earning the customer's business. The operational side of the business helps earn the customers' business and keeps them coming back time and again.

Many companies are created, get busy, grow, and then reach a plateau. By that time, they are so set in their ways that changing even to improve is difficult. People often get used to doing something a certain way; they say "this is how it's done" or "it's always been this way." But "it" doesn't have to be that way.

Since you are most likely at the very beginning of starting your business, you have the opportunity to set the high standard of becoming a great company. Set the tone and the expected work ethics to establish excellent customer service and to deliver a quality product to your customers, all so that those customers will want to spend their hard-earned money on you.

One of the most mundane tasks is documenting your business processes and creating training manuals for your company. The mind-set of some entrepreneurs is that they do not have time for this. If you have this mind-set, your employees will too. But to ensure that your business operation runs smoothly and that other people know what is expected, you need to document every aspect. Create business based rules that will help you manage your work process flow. Business rules such as if this then that scenario will help your employees understand why things are done a certain way.

The biggest benefit to creating this knowledge base is that the process helps you truly understand how your business operates. This also helps your employees understand their job responsibilities. In addition, if someone is out because of sickness or vacation, someone else can step up and fill in as needed.

For example, in my previous business, in every workstation, the daily, weekly, and monthly tasks were posted. This made accomplishing the day's primary tasks easier for all employees.

A documented system helps mitigate the negative impact of the key employee leaving your company. Without documented procedures, when employees leave your company, they may take their knowledge and leave you in a lurch. With an updated knowledge base and a well-documented work process, you can sleep better at night, knowing that everything is organized.

The success of a business doesn't rest solely on the uniqueness of its products; it lies on its execution of bringing the product into the marketplace. The execution is its business process and is the key to success.

Back-End Operations

First, you should document any kind of back-end operations process, such as an inventory management system. Some ecommerce solutions provide back-end features, but I prefer to have an integrated accounting, inventory and order management system, CRM such as NetSuite or Brightpearl.com.

Other more affordable solutions, such as Stone Edge Technology (SEOM), can also work nicely. Although Stone Edge does not have an accounting capability, it offers enough that you can export summary data into QuickBooks or another similar accounting software. Other third-party solutions that work nicely with SEOM can also help you understand your data better in order to grow your business. If you are planning to open a retail store as well, make sure to find a solution that will grow with your business, both online and brick-and-mortar.

Find out what type of training support your solution provider will be giving you along with your purchase. The biggest consideration is not just the initial software acquisition cost but the cost of maintaining your system. One of your primary goals is to have a knowledge management system to house all your company's process documentations. This will help with you with training your current and future employees on any back-end systems you choose to use.

Factor in work hours spent learning the process. In one situation we got ourselves into, we had to hire a person at forty thousand dollars a year just to ensure that the journal entries were being posted into the correct category every night. What a waste of time and energy! Be sure to really understand how the software works, as well as what type of workarounds there will be if you are replacing an existing system. If you are brand new, walk through the workflow to determine what you will need in terms of labor to get the task or work done.

When documenting your workflow, keep in mind that the fewer times a person is required to touch an order, the better. Ensure that your process is efficient. This should be your goal with every touch point; the order process moves forward to fulfilling the customer's order.

Since people learn differently and most are visual, flowcharts and screenshots that include each step are very helpful as training material. Your employees will be more focused on the material rather than on taking complete notes.

Benefits of a Documented Step-by-Step Workflow

- Provides training materials for new employees
- Provides reminders of procedures and the order of how things are to be completed
- Can help you see the gaps in your process, steps that are inefficient, areas of weakness, or areas prone to human error. This will help you define the problem so you can find a solution.
- Helps employees see how each task is interdependent with coworkers' tasks; provides a better understanding of work linkage and cooperation between employees and departments, especially in areas where there are clear handoffs
- Helps you understand your labor costs and productivity, so you can determine when you should add more people, where you can optimize processes, and when you can be more efficient
- Ensures that each step being completed is adding value to the customer, rather than being done for the sake of being a busybody
- Reduces human errors and provides a consistently positive customer experience
- Helps you and your employees work on the most important aspect of your business; it helps you to prioritize
- Brings you peace of mind as a business owner
- Encourage information sharing and free flow of information within your company

Writing out your work process at the start of your business is easier than backtracking, even if you need to tweak things along the way. As your business grows, your day-to-day tasks will likely be delegated to employees, so having the steps on paper will be beneficial.

Include the time required for each task, when applicable. In addition, for every task that involves several steps, write down the purpose of each step, the time to complete each, and the desired outcome before moving to the next step. This will help future employees understand the importance of what they are working on and why.

Review the process on a regular basis. This will help you track productivity and find ways to improve your process; it will also give you an indicator of when to add more employees and what labor cost is associated with each task.

A common complaint that I hear from business owners about employees is that they are not getting things done properly. Ironically, the most common task an owner does is train and retrain new employees on the same task over and over again—basically, teaching the same thing over and over again to new people. Talk about wasting valuable time! And the problem is that the training process is not documented properly.

Some common problems are customers complaining about orders, either because something is not right or not delivered; in response, employees often end up pointing fingers at one another.

When I come across these scenarios as a consultant, I always question the process before the employee. I ensure that the procedure and work process are in place, tested, reviewed, and set up correctly to eliminate errors. If you have vetted the process properly and most employees are able to complete the task correctly, the ones who fall short are either not trained properly or inadequate. But you won't know unless you have a proven procedure in place.

Management Tips

- Each employee needs to have a clear, detailed job description.
- Create benchmarks and success metrics to measure, track, and monitor the employee.
- Ensure that the employee understands and accepts his or her accountability and responsibility to the job. Clear expectations must be defined up front to avoid confusion and misunderstandings.
- If an employee is not working out, let him or her go. You are not doing the employee any favors by keeping him or her around. Keeping nonproductive employees will only cause distractions, which may lower overall employee morale.
- Create a working environment in which employees are passionately dedicated to winning in the marketplace.
- Once your store has launched, be diligent about optimizing your daily operations.

- Always ask yourself and your team on how you can serve your customers better, cheaper, and faster as a continuing effort of improving your company.

Key tactical activities:

- Add new and exciting products.
- Reorder your best sellers.
- Get rid of slow sellers and dead inventory.
- Process orders and ship them in a timely manner.
- Keep in touch with the customer regarding order status.
- Stay on top of customer service issues.
- Manage merchandise returns.
- Monitor daily updates and regularly test your website.
- Continuously engage customers and market to them.
- Maintain and update financial records.

Chapter 18.

Customer Service: Catch Hell or Outshine and Outsell the Competition

You will go to Ecom Hell if: *you do not like dealing with customers.*

There is only one boss. The customer. And he can fire everybody in the company from the chairman on down, simply by spending his money somewhere else.

—Sam Walton

Customers are people. Some people can be very easy to get along with, while others, not so much. In business, most customers will be happy with your company, but some will not be. If you understand this, then focusing on providing solutions to the problem, instead of thinking that the customer is always wrong, will make your life easier. Do not vilify your customers, even when they are wrong and are trying to take advantage of you. They just want to get the maximum value for their money. Can you blame them for that?

Customer Service

Every company is expected to have good customer service. But in today's competitive marketplace, great customer service can be a differentiator, especially when you are selling commodity goods (i.e., stuff everyone else can sell).

Great customer service begins with good website design and is determined by a satisfied customer. If your website design is friendly, easy to use, and intuitive, you will be less likely to get calls from frustrated customers.

To continue to achieve great customer service, your people, processes, and products must all exist to make the customer happy. Focus on your customers' needs. Design your business flow so that it serves your customers best, even if what is required is not always the easiest path for you.

Your customer service department is the front line to customers. Customer service representatives (CSRs) should be good listeners who are empathetic and who can convey company policies diplomatically. Be sure to notify your CSRs of any changes in policy, service, pricing, products, or order-processing times (often due to seasonal demand). Make sure that CSRs also know of any special marketing campaigns or promotions (don't let them find out when a customer calls to ask about the promotion). Customer service can make or break your company. Any negative dealings your customers have with your CSRs may end up as complaints to the Better Business Bureau or, worse, the online community.

Include a business phone number on your website. Some people still prefer to make payments or ask questions over the phone.

Use customer complaints to improve your customer service practices. Dealing with complaints gives you an opportunity to resolve issues and, in some cases, to turn an angry customer into a raving fan. A phone conversation gives customers a more personal touch, assuring them that a complaint is heard and that they will be taken seriously.

Sometimes a customer's complaint lingers as conversation within a department. Discourage this type of discussion, especially if this is simply someone complaining about a customer complaining. This unproductive talk only leads to low morale and unnecessary stress. Instead, encourage a conversation that focuses on providing solutions. Once solutions have been found and implemented, that should be the end of the conversation.

Staff your call center with capable CSRs, who are armed with clearly defined policies for handling most situations. Knowing the most common reasons for why customers call can help you prepare appropriate responses (use flexible scripts for consistency). Post your policies in a conspicuous place on your website, and offer frequently asked questions (FAQs) to answer a majority of customer inquiries. Your call center will be more streamlined and effective if simple questions are answered online. For added convenience, offer an online chat, click to call, or email contact form to communicate with your customers. All of these solutions offer a way to track and manage incoming emails and calls.

One example of customer service issue is when order processing is behind schedule and the shipment went out late. Do you upgrade the shipment from ground to an air shipment? Is this a shipping issue or is this a CSR issue? Only your business base rules can really answer that, but whichever is the answer, make sure your CSRs are prepared.

This is usually the time I get asked about outsourcing. There are instances when outsourcing makes sense. For example, my company outsourced our after-hours call center so that our customers could speak to a live agent at any time. You have to determine what make sense for your business, but remember to always be serving your customers.

Customer Service Do's

- Resolve issues promptly.
- Return customer calls, within the same day if possible.
- Role-play customer service call scenarios as part of your CSR training.
- Create policies and scripts for CSRs to use for routine calls.
- Periodically audit customer service calls.
- Log queries and types of calls. Populate your FAQs page with the most common queries. (Redact customers' personal data or any identifying information.)

- Add a personal touch through handwritten notes, especially when communicating about cancelled orders, returns, credit, etc.
- Follow through on promises.
- In addition, managers and owners should personally take CSR calls every few months, just to keep engaged and have direct interaction with customers. This is always helpful in understanding what your business is about and further helps you understand your customer base.
- Have written policies that your CSR's can easily understand and follow.
- Ensure that you develop a business process to respond to each type of customer communication such as emails, phone calls and even mail.
- Train CSRs to understand product attributes and benefits.

Customer Service Don'ts

- Don't promise something unless you can do it.
- Don't keep someone on hold forever.
- Don't make customers have to navigate a phone tree nightmare.
- Don't resolve issues case by case; instead, try to formalize new policies for common issues.
- Don't give customers the runaround for anything, especially refunds.
- Don't hide behind your policy.
- Don't take customer complaints personally.
- Don't lose your temper—ever.

Most Common Complaints about Ecommerce Companies

- The product did not arrive or did not arrive on time or as promised.
- The customer was put on hold for a long time.
- No one called or emailed back after the customer left a message.
- The CSR was rude or argumentative.

- The customer was given incorrect information (e.g., about the product, procedure, company policies, etc).
- The refunds or credit was not issued properly or in a timely manner.
- The order was lost.
- The company did not provide up-to-date status on a late shipment.
- The company cancelled an order without notification or without providing alternative choices or recommendations.
- The employee hid behind "stated company policy."
- The retail store advertised price was not honored.

Most Common Reasons for Customer Calls

- To check on order status.
- To check on shipping status.
- To question an invoice or the amount charged.
- To obtain the shipping tracking number.
- To check on the status of a refund.
- To report a product that arrived damaged.
- To obtain the return authorization number.

Questions to Ask Yourself about Your Customer Service

- Are our employees friendly, courteous, attentive, and responsive to customers' needs?
- Are our employees knowledgeable about our products? Do they understand customers' needs?
- How can we improve every interaction with customers? How do we move them from just being satisfied to being wowed?
- How quickly and professionally do we respond to complaints or issues raised by our customers?
- How often do we follow through and audit our product quality control?
- Are we providing enough product information and support on the merchandise we sell?
- Would our customers recommend us to a friend or their family members? Why or why not?

Order Processing: "Show Me the Money"

Order processing is literally your money department. That is where you will bring in your hard-earned dollars. But you have to fulfill the orders before you can make your way happily to the bank.

Processing orders should be done every day. Process two or three batches at different times of the day, depending on how you run your operation. We used to process once in the morning right when we got in at around 9:00 a.m. and again at 1:00 p.m. By breaking orders into batches, we were able to process rush orders and air shipment orders first. Then, we would process all the drop-ship orders, especially to meet East Coast vendors' cutoff time.

Be sure that the tracking number from your shipping gets entered back into your order management software. Ideally, this should be a seamless process that does not require manually entering data more than once. Your customer should be able to track the shipment online according to the order number; this will cut down on customer service calls.

The best advice I can offer regarding order processing is to be consistent in your procedures. Develop a systematic procedure that you and your staff follow every day. Resist the urge to take shortcuts. Always follow up with the customer when you are unable to process an order for any reason. Use the checklist below as a guide for what should be included in your best practice procedures.

Order Processing Checklist

☐ Process orders consistently at around the same time every day and/or have specified cut-ff time.

☐ Notify customers right away if you're unable to process an order.

☐ Notify customers through your shopping cart to confirm that you have received their order.

☐ Create email templates for customer notification during instances when products are out of stock,the shipment is delayed, or when an item is backordered.

☐ Notify customers when orders will be shipped from multiple warehouses and when shipment dates will be different from the stated information on your website.

☐ Notify customers when there are partial shipments or when orders are not shipped completely in one shipment.

☐ Email customers right away once you have tracking numbers for their orders. Provide multiple tracking numbers if shipments are shipped separately.

☐ Authorize the credit card for the transaction amount first, before you finish processing the order. There are federal laws requiring you to ship goods before you can charge the card. Authorization merely reserves the amount to be charged.

☐ Develop and adhere to processing rules regarding address verification system (AVS) and CVV numbers. The AVS number ensures that the ship-to address matches the credit card billing address. The CVV number is the three- or four-digit number that appears on the back of credit cards as a security measure.

Fraud Prevention

As an online business, you might encounter fraudulent orders. Although you cannot eliminate fraud completely, you can reduce your exposure. Sometimes, the fraudsters' intent is not for you to ship the order; instead, they are just looking for a way to find out what the credit limit is on a credit card. Therefore, set procedures in place to catch these incidents. However, do not get too caught up in worrying about this, as fraud orders are relatively infrequent.

One word of caution—ensure that your back end is PCI compliant. Do not keep credit card numbers on file if you really don't need to. Also ensure that any sensitive information about your customers is encrypted in your system, just in case security is compromised.

There are also fraud subscription services. Although these can be expensive for smaller companies, if you are selling high-end products, it is worth looking into the cost. These services can verify the customer's IP and determine whether fraud activity has been associated with particular IP addresses. They can also check whether the IP address of a credit card owner is domestic or international.

Fraud Checklist

☐ Pay attention to the order value. Note any orders that are significantly higher than usual (in amount or quantity).

☐ Watch for next-day air or overnight orders. Review these to ensure that the AVS and CVV numbers match up. If you're suspicious, call the customer or check the Internet to verify the address.

☐ Watch for multiple transactions from the same IP address using different credit cards.

☐ Pay attention to orders for big-ticket products.

☐ Note any unusual repeat orders.

Returns, Exchanges, and Money-Back Guarantees

A money-back guarantee is standard practice in ecommerce. Everyone, including your competition, is offering one. Although this is not a UVP (unique value proposition) to say that you offer this feature, if you do not offer one (or a similar guarantee), it will cause you to lose business.

The question is how will you execute the policy? Will your guarantee be within thirty days from receipt, sixty or ninety days, or even 365 days, like Zappos?

If you could call it "the happiness guarantee," what would that program look like?

People shop online even though the return process can be difficult. Keep customers coming back to you by making returns easy. This actually makes it easy for you and your employees too. Do not make customers jump through lots of hoops. The more hoops they go through, the more steps you have to enforce for something that, in the end, will only hurt your brand. Instead, provide a clear, written return policy and spell out the rules for returns. Provide a return-shipping label on all orders (you'll only pay if an item is returned).

To avoid confusion when refunds are issued, be sure to issue the refund to the same credit card the purchase was originally charged against. Handle all chargebacks promptly. If your company experiences numerous chargebacks, your account can get dinged. This means you could lose the ability to accept credit cards. So be vigilant in protecting your company's credit standing.

There are so many reasons why products get returned. These are some of the reasons that I or my clients experienced in their business: Incorrect item, incorrect quantity, duplicate order, arrived too late, didn't order the item, incorrect shipping address, customer ordered the wrong item or wrong size or it's damaged. Whatever the reason may be, you want to understand that it is basically just a part of doing business online. What is important to focus on is making it easy for the customer to return the goods and for your company to develop an efficient business process to deal with the returns.

Managing Returns and Exchanges

Returns and exchanges can be one of the least exciting aspects of running your business, but they are necessary. Managing returns includes returns of unwanted or damaged merchandise and merchandise exchanged for something else. Be sure to communicate policies and procedures for dealing with returned merchandise and returns to your vendor or drop shipper.

My previous company's policy was not to accept returns on any personalized or monogrammed product, unless they were damaged or defective upon receipt. Nonpersonalized products returned because they were not what the customers wanted could be returned within thirty days. Issue a return tracking number when a customer calls to return an item, and log this number into the customer notes in your order management software. Once the package is returned to the warehouse, process the paperwork to accounting so it can be verified against the customer account and the customer credit can be issued.

My previous company had a good relationship with our drop shippers, who were willing to take back products for straight return and credit, as well as replacement for damaged and defective products. The key to managing returns with drop shippers is to track goods returned by customers and to ensure that credit gets issued to customers on time. Track returns to drop shippers on an in-house return form that is then sent to accounting so they can reconcile the transaction against the customer's account and match this against the vendor's invoice. If the invoice has been paid already, wait for a credit to be issued. If the invoice has not been paid, email or include in your monthly payment schedule those invoices with pending credit against them.

Merchandise Return Checklist

☐ Provide an online return system that automatically issues a return merchandise authorization (RMA) number. Provide an RMA form with a preprinted address label that the customer can affix to a return box.

☐ Include an instruction sheet for returns with every order shipment.

☐ Provide a preprinted return label if you're covering the return shipment cost (you only have to pay the postage if the item is actually returned).

☐ Don't have a customer return a product that you can't resell again (e.g., personalized items). Instead, issue a credit and ask the customer to discard the merchandise.

☐ Set up a way to get rid of returns outside your store, such as an eBay store, for returns only where you can sell it below retail to recover some of your cost.

☐ Calculate the number of personnel hours spent processing returns to figure out what your dollar threshold should be for taking back physical returns from a customer. If a return item is under that dollar amount, don't worry about having it sent back. Consider issuing the credit and call it a loss, as it will likely cost you more in postage and merchandise handling.

☐ Create a separate area in your warehouse for returns to be processed daily to ensure that credit is issued to customers in a timely manner.

☐ Arrange a pickup service with a liquidator or a nonprofit for merchandise that you can't resell. Be sure to keep an itemized record for tax purposes.

☐ Scrap or destroy and write off low-value merchandise and have it removed from your warehouse, since it's likely taking up valuable physical space and limiting your ability to bring in fresh inventory.

☐ Address underlying issues. If a certain item is being returned frequently, it may need to be eliminated or the quality of the vendor may need to be examined.

☐ If a customer calls in for an RMA number or to ask about returning an item, try to save the order by enticing the customer to keep the product at a reduced price. Then credit the customer the necessary amount.

☐ Use the customer's call to understand the reason for returns and to increase your knowledge of how customers are interacting with your website, your company, and your products.

☐ Set a procedure to follow up with vendor / drop shipper returns as well as for returns from your own warehouse.

Warehousing

Inventory is the largest investment most companies have on the books. Ordering and stocking just enough inventory to meet customer demands (a.k.a. just-in-time or JIT inventory management) is the key to managing your inventory levels and cash flow effectively. Make sure to maximize warehouse space. Avoid "sitting" on cash by liquidating slow sellers and removing dead inventory; this will also lower your holding costs.

As orders increase, so will the potential for errors, and this can affect customer service and satisfaction. Your primary goal is accuracy. Reduce the chance for errors and increase efficiency by maintaining an organized warehouse. Focus on cost per order, aging inventory, SKU counts, returns due to packing errors, inventory damage value, and reducing touch points.

Keep your best sellers near your packers. Make sure that bins and shelves are marked clearly with the item code, and, whenever possible, post the same photos for products that you use on the web. Name the item exactly the way the name is printed on the picking list or invoice.

Create one area for receiving, another for damaged goods, another for return-to-vendor (RTV) items, and another for returns from customers. This will help keep your warehouse more organized and will enable you to see which areas need immediate attention.

Sort all pick tickets by aisle to save your pickers time and to keep aisles clear for safety compliance and efficiency. Train staff on workplace safety, and reward them for compliance. Double-check what is being packed (ideally, the picker should not be the packer) to ensure accuracy.

Staff your warehouse with both full-time and part-time employees in the event of short bursts of increased sales. Labor costs are your largest expense in warehouse management.

Warehouse Checklist

☐ Keep your best sellers near your packers.

☐ Make sure that bins and shelves are marked clearly with the item code and with the same photo used on the web. Name the item exactly as it is printed on the picking list or invoice.

☐ Keep your warehouse organized by having separate areas for receiving, damaged goods, return-to-vendor (RTV) items, and returns from customers. This will also enable you to see which areas need immediate attention.

☐ Sort your pick tickets by aisle to save your pickers time.

☐ Keep aisles clear and organized, not only for safety compliance, but also to make it more efficient for your pickers.

☐ Have a double-check system for what is being packed to help avoid customer complaints and prevent returns. Your picker generally should not be your packer.

☐ Train for warehouse safety and provide incentives and rewards. For example, have a pizza party for "No reported injuries for thirty days."

☐ Reduce touch points. The fewer times a product is handled, the lower the cost of shipping. Review your systems and processes and streamline as much as possible.

☐ In addition to full-time packers and pickers, have part-time employees available for any short bursts of increased sales.

Inventory Loss Prevention

In this case, inventory loss prevention refers to merchandise lost through theft or damage. No matter how good your inventory software is, it alone cannot eliminate loss due to theft or mishandling. However, you are actually more likely to suffer merchandise loss due to waste and misplacement than theft. If you are selling high-value products, be sure to keep them under lock and key. They should be released only under proper authorization or by a select number of authorized employees.

Most merchandise is lost through carelessness. Products can be damaged by poor methods of holding or storage. Shelving may be inadequate or poorly designed, or the merchandise may be exposed to the elements and become unsellable. Take extra care to walk through your warehouse to ensure that merchandise is packed and stacked properly. Store light-colored items and fabric materials in protective clear plastic bags away from direct sunlight. For example, if you are in the apparel business, make sure boxes are protected from dust, sunlight, and moisture. Reduce risk of damage by avoiding eating and other messy activities in the merchandise area. Isolate hazardous and flammable materials or chemicals from stored merchandise. I used to tell employees that merchandise on the shelf is like having a stack of money that needs to be taken care of and kept safe.

Loss Prevention Tips

- Don't stack heavy products on light ones.
- Keep shelving units organized and clean.
- Keep high-value products under lock and key.
- Keep merchandise protected from outside elements.
- Rotate inventory by using the first-in/first-out (FIFO) method. Do not stack recently received shipments in front of older inventory.

Shipping

For an online store that sells goods, shipping is critical, so work with reliable shipping partners. Most ecommerce businesses use more than one service; for example, my previous company used both UPS and FedEx for outbound shipments.

If there is room in your budget, incorporate shipping-rate comparison tools in your website, as these can help you save money right from the beginning. Shipping cost is an area that can become a runaway freight train, so get control of your costs right from the beginning. Any money you save will add to your company's profitability.

Make sure your shipping process is seamless, easy, and logical. Set your packing material, such as boxes, packing tape, and packing popcorn, within steps of where your orders are packed. Packing tables should be organized and well stocked with supplies.

As mentioned earlier, have separate staff for pulling orders and for packing orders, as this saves time and provides a double-check system to ensure orders are correct. Another time-saving strategy is to pick and pack similar merchandise at the same time, as it's easier to mass-produce boxes of the same size and pack them than to randomly build different sizes of packing boxes.

The packer/shipper should never be more than two feet from his or her packing station. To save on costs, it is important to run a very tight shipping process. Focus on how many boxes are packed in an hour and how many are shipped in a day. Place the packer and all boxes for pickup near the doorway where UPS/FedEx picks up and drops off shipments. This way, you can keep packing and processing shipments up to the very last minute, even as UPS counts and loads the other boxes into the truck.

You may be thinking that you want to outsource your shipping and fulfillment tasks. Of course, there are advantages and disadvantages to this. Outsourcing these tasks will make managing daily shipping and inventory easier. This will most likely cost a little less than if you were doing the shipping. This is because these companies have economies of scale. Some fulfillment centers also operate a customer call center to handle shipping-related questions. These companies often have a more efficient back end that can easily integrate with your front-end system. However, a downside of outsourcing is that you have less control over how your orders are packaged and shipped. This could possibly lead to upset customers and more headaches for you, as well as increase your costs and erode your profits. Another disadvantage could occur if the company has other, bigger customers who take priority over you.

Whether you pack your items or some other company does, the more times an item is handled, the more this costs you and the more chances there are for errors or damaged goods. In this case, efficiency can lead to cost savings.

Shipping productivity should be measured on customer satisfaction, even as the goal is to increase outbound shipments. If you get lots of returns due to damaged goods packed by your staff, reassess your packing methods. When customers receive their order, they should feel like they are opening a gift. One of the most important touch points is when the customer receives a package from you. If your goods arrive broken or not carefully and thoughtfully packaged, you leave a negative impression that extends to your brand. When you can stir a positive emotional connection, however, you have achieved your goal—a happy customer!

I am not going to cover shipping internationally because it's pretty complex and loaded with paperwork. I recommend that when you start getting inquiries from international base customers that you partner up with a reliable freight carrier or shipper to help you with the shipment process. Look into shipping companies like Bongo.com to expand your business internationally.

The Two Sides of the Shipping Quandary

Shipping as a Profit Center

A few years ago, I viewed shipping charges as a profit center. They definitely added to our bottom line and helped us recover the ever-increasing costs we paid to UPS, FedEx, and the US Postal Service. But the competitive nature of my industry changed my view about this. We tried different formulas, like charging a flat rate of $9.95 when the order was under $100.00 and free shipping on purchases over $100.00. But eventually, we figured out that we broke even around $150.00, because some of our products were pretty heavy when purchased in large quantities. I was fine with breaking even on shipping and even subsidizing it a little bit so that we could grow our sales. The important thing for you is to figure out your top line sales growth based on giving away free shipping.

Whether or not free or subsidized shipping is right for you is based largely on profit margin, conversion rate, and average dollar purchased. During the holidays, your site will experience increased traffic, so this is the best time to check (test this) where your breakeven point is or if your profit level will increase if you give away or subsidize shipping.

Shipping Gotchas

Always be sure to review your shipper's statement so you have a strong handle on what you're being billed for. It's not uncommon to see outbound shipping total costs that are about 24 to 26 percent of your revenue! Here are some of the shipping "gotchas" that will result to additional expenses charge to your company.

- Extra shipping charge for address corrections
- Charge for oversized packages
- Charge for Saturday delivery
- Charge for residential delivery
- Special undelivered surcharges

This is another reason that having shipping comparison software is important, as it helps you compare rates at the point of shipment to keep costs down.

Shipping Tips

- Insure packages. Set a dollar value that you're willing to take the hit for. UPS automatically insures for one hundred dollars of coverage, but they will only pay the replacement value, not the retail invoice value. You may want to consider self-insurance, as this can help reduce your monthly shipping cost.
- Keep track of how many packages go out daily.
- Track the productivity of each shipping employee. For example, Employee Y can pack and ship x boxes in an hour, multiplied by eight hours = ?

- Make your shipping process seamless and easy for employees to follow.
- Do not trade efficiency purely for saving money; you run the risk of poor packaging, errors, or increased damaged goods.
- Keep a separate journal entry in accounting for inbound and outbound shipping costs. Lumping everything into one expense will prevent you from seeing your true outbound shipping costs. If you are providing free shipping, you will not know how much you are giving away to attract orders.
- Use environmentally friendly packing materials.

Shipping Department Checklist

☐ Keep packing supplies and boxes near the packing station.

☐ Include promotional materials with each shipment.

☐ Include return forms and preprinted address labels that can be affixed to a box for easy return.

☐ Consider self-insuring for shipments exceeding a hundred dollars in value.

☐ Use clean, new boxes for shipment.

☐ Create a feeling of "opening a gift" for your customer.

☐ Provide sufficient packing material to reduce potential for damage.

☐ Keep track of daily shipment productivity and set goals for your employees.

☐ Provide your staff with the necessary tools to be successful in achieving their goals.

☐ Reduce the number of touch points for inventory: fewer touches = higher profits.

☐ Provide tracking order tools on your website, as this will reduce calls to your company. Ensure that your back end sends the tracking information to your website. Shipment confirmation, order confirmation, and thank-you emails should also contain links to a "track your order" page so that customers can easily find it. There can never be too much communication with your customers; only undercommunication can lead to problems.

Chapter 19.

Human Resources

You will go to Ecom Hell if: *you do not trust (if you micromanage) your employees.*

As your business grows, you'll need to hire employees. Choosing the right employees is important to your success. You will have to learn to trust your employees and provide them with the autonomy to make decisions on your behalf. Knowing how to hire, retain, and develop your employees will be pivotal to whether your company lives or dies.

If your company is large enough, you might need to create a human resources department. Whether you are the HR person (and owner, manager, CEO, etc) or you hire staff for this, the responsibilities are the same: hire staff, assist with business flow creation for each department, create job descriptions, and handle payroll and personnel issues (e.g., employee development, maternity leave, and health-care administration). Be sure to document everything related to your employees (W-2, I-9 forms, applications, résumés) in an organized fashion, and keep these files under lock and key.

Hire only when you have to, and hire the best you can afford. Do not hire someone and expect him or her to learn on their own. Make sure you understand exactly what the job requires and demonstrate the task to your new hire (or have detailed task descriptions for him or her to follow). The saying goes, "Hire slow and fire fast." If someone is not working out, you are not doing that person any favors by keeping him or her around. If you are unsure about someone, hire the person as temp-to-permanent (start as an independent contractor for a month to three months). If that works out, you can hire the person permanently.

In addition to a job-training manual, create and distribute a company handbook containing information on what your company is about, benefits, paid holidays, and company policy (e.g., cell phone use, protocol for handling conflicts and other issues like absenteeism). Ask employees to read your handbook and sign off on it.

Create a training program for each department. Ensure that all training materials are current and frequently updated. Do not conduct training on the fly, or you'll set your employee up for failure. It's best to create an inexpensive company intranet where documents such as these can be stored, easily shared, and updated. As your company grows, you will need to give training a high priority (including making time, resources, and capital available) so that your employees will have an up-to-date skill set that will help you continue to grow your company. I also recommend creating a pathway for your employees to grow within your organization by implementing a professional development program that encourages employees to pick up new skills.

If you can, conduct biannual job reviews, giving both positive feedback and constructive criticism. Give praise in public, and criticize (positively) in private. Focus on collaboration and not competition, as nobody wins when employees are pitted against one another. Provide a detailed job description that includes key responsibilities and what bonuses and salary increases will be based upon.

You may want to farm out your payroll processing. We contracted ours to Paychex Inc. because we did not want the responsibility of having to keep up with federal payroll laws. Another good reason to sign up with a third party is that they shoulder the responsibility and then remedy any incorrect payroll tax filing.

Hiring Tips

- Present a complete, detailed job description to prospective hires to give them an idea of what the job truly entails. This sets the tone for expectations and should minimize the "I didn't know that" comments later on.
- With each job description, indicate what a successful metric would be. For example, the employee is successful at this job if he or she achieves/completes, turns out, produces x widgets, reports, sales, etc. Defining success upfront will set the focus on the employee's responsibilities and goals.
- With each job description, create primary and secondary responsibilities. Primary (e.g., help customers) is the employee's main focus. Secondary (e.g., clean the shelves) is any adjunct supporting role that is required of the employee to help a coworker or department get things done.
- Create an employee profile of the type of employees you want. You can base this on your own personality type or that of the owner/founder/current employees. As you add new employees, this profile can be the initial filter to check for compatibility. It can help you avoid anyone who is not a good fit or wouldn't make it in the long run.
- Hire for ability. Some candidates will interview really well, because they have read all the interview books, know what questions will be asked, and are rehearsed and well-practiced. But are they capable of doing the job?
- Conduct a phone interview first. I like to interview a person on the phone as an initial contact. This keeps me from getting sidetracked by first impressions based on appearances.
- Always verify candidates' references. Ask references open-ended questions, as they are less rehearsed than the interviewee and would be more willing to share. Ask about the candidates' best strengths and weaknesses. Ask the question: in what work situation did this quality arise or was put to the test?
- Hire candidates who like working with people. Teamwork cannot be underestimated. Candidates who demonstrate team spirit (or

who have been part of team sports in the past) are ideal, as they are more likely to know how to get along with others.

- Look for qualities like leadership, character, discipline, persistence, and self-motivation.
- For additional information, check out Lou Adler's *Hiring with Your Head* and Bradford Smart's *Top Grading*.

Human Resources Checklist

☐ Have the employee fill out an employment application and provide a résumé.

☐ Check references and verify a potential employee's employment history.

☐ Create and distribute individual job descriptions and an employee handbook to each employee.

☐ Obtain the following documents from each employee and keep them secured.

1. Signed I-9 Form (Employment Eligibility Verification)

2. Signed W-4 Form (Employee Withholding Certificate)

3. Copy of driver's license for employee file (optional)

4. Unemployment insurance tax registration (if necessary)

5. Copy of Social Security card

☐ Maintain an employee access checklist that lists usernames and passwords that you give each employee. This will help you recall what employees have access to in the event that you terminate someone.

Chapter 20.

To Hell and Gone: Accounting

You will go to Ecom Hell if: *you do not keep accurate and timely records.*

Because entrepreneurs are so focused on revenue, accounting is one of the most overlooked departments in small businesses, whether brick-and-mortar or ecommerce.

If you get behind in your bookkeeping, you will experience "hell and gone" to catch up again, if you can. Proper bookkeeping helps you know the health of your business. With accurate books, you can manage and run your business properly, knowing where you stand and eliminating worry.

This allows you to focus on doing a better job for your customers. At the end of the day, it's not how much you sell, but how much you keep. You can sell a million dollars, but if you spent a million and one dollars to operate your business, you are still not profitable. Focus on being profitable, not just your top line revenue.

If you are a new to starting a business, then you have a blank slate on which to get this right. Be sure to talk to an accountant to help you set up your accounting books. The fee is worth having a professional accountant set this up for you. Work with the accountant to determine what type of business entity you have and to set up your chart of accounts accordingly.

You will also need to choose cash or accrual accounting. In fact, once your business reaches a certain dollar amount, you will have to go with the accrual accounting method.

If you are looking for a new back-end system, make sure your accountant ensures that the accounting processes of the new system work with your accounting system. If there are certain processes that do not match up, you might want to identify them and create a step-by-step process (workaround) to get there.

If you are already in business, review the current state of your books. Are you up-to-date on your bank reconciliation, credit card reconciliation, payroll updates, and the like? Do you have a budget set up for each of your accounts? Make sure to include your revenue forecast and expense projections (business plan). Then go back and enter the actual revenue and expenses to see how close you are to the budgeted (projected) numbers to make sure that you are on track. This exercise can greatly affect your cash flow and help you see any areas in which you can continue to invest to add to your bottom line. If you are not profitable, this opens your eyes to the areas that are bleeding money and need fixing.

Make sure you are reviewing your updated financial statements every month. Focus on the balance sheet, the profit and loss (P&L) report, and the cash-flow statement. On your balance sheet, focus in particular on where your money is being held. Is it cash in the bank or inventory and equipment (assets)? For the P&L, pay attention to your sales revenue and your cost of goods sold (COGS). Review margins monthly to identify anomalies. Review your expenses monthly and compare each month's expenses with the same period of the previous year to ensure that nothing unexplainable is going on.

A cash-flow statement helps you determine whether you have enough cash to sustain your operations through slower months and invest wisely during peak months. Your monthly expenses and monthly revenue are allocated here, along with details of cash receipts and cash outlays not listed on the P&L. What you're looking for in your cash-flow statement is positive cash flow (making more money than your business is using). When your company consistently has more cash in the bank than you are reporting on your P&L, this is a sign that you have a good cash reserve. But you also want to ensure that you are leveraging your cash asset by investing in more inventory to sell (as an example) and turning a profit once again. In other words, you are making money with your money.

Accounting Tips

- Track and monitor all your revenue and expenses, as this helps you pay bills on time, manage cash flow, and determine whether you have the funds to invest in things like equipment needed to grow your business. Not managing accounting data properly may lead you to make poor or incorrect choices/decisions.
- Make sure your accounting data is up-to-date and accurate. Review your journal entries every month to ensure entries are properly categorized.
- Make sure you have at least six months of operating cash flow. The only time your cash flow should be low is toward the end of your slow season when you're expecting your busy season to kick in just in time to replenish your cash reserves. Just because there is money in the bank doesn't mean that you are doing well. Monthly review and monitoring allows you the flexibility to react and take action quickly if things are not going according to plan.

Accounting Tips for Working with Drop Shippers

- If you only have a few transactions per vendor, it might be better to pay by credit card. Have your drop shipper charge you per invoice so that it's easier to match up against the credit card statement when you reconcile.
- If you have a lot of transactions, work with your vendor to create a file that you upload to your back-end system. This will save you time and money in manually handling the invoices one by one.
- Follow up on credits and returns right away. Do not let them pile up, as it will be difficult to recall the facts and details of each order as time passes.

- If your account is on credit terms, inform your vendor right away to avoid a freeze on your account. Work out a payment schedule amenable to both your needs.
- Inform your vendor of any reasons why you might skip or refuse to pay an invoice. Settle disputed invoices and payments quickly. Do not let this fester, as it will deteriorate any goodwill that you have built up.

Tips for Invoices

If you have thirty or more orders that need to be entered each day, you should check with your back-end vendor to see if certain entries can be uploaded automatically. Uploading invoices or orders minimizes errors. It may be time to consider having your front system (website) send orders to your back-end system.

Accounting Department Checklist

☐ Create the following reports:

1. A daily sales and bank deposit report that includes a comparison of daily revenue with the previous year's
2. A weekly report on profitability, with margins by category
3. A cash flow report that you compare monthly against department and category budgets
4. A daily report on how many boxes were shipped
5. A daily report on the number of back orders and their dollar value.

☐ Reconcile the following:

1. Monthly credit card statements against invoices
2. Monthly bank statements against deposits and checks issued
3. Bank deposits against credit-card batches of the prior day/s
4. Purchase orders against vendor billings

☐ Tackle chargebacks, dispute letters, and credit refunds immediately.

☐ Pay all accounts payable and bills promptly.

☐ Collect/bill all invoices that are due to your company in a timely manner.

☐ Separate your personal finances from your business (credit cards, checking accounts).

☐ Collect and pay appropriate sales and use taxes.

☐ Create procedures to handle credit card chargebacks (i.e., when a customer calls the credit card company to dispute charges).

Five Common Chargeback Scenarios

1. The customer changed his or her mind, but you refused to give credit; the customer then disputed the order with the credit card company.
2. The customer claims to have never received the goods/shipment. This could be due to any of the following:
    *   Lost by carrier
    *   Left on the front porch and stolen
    *   You forgot to ship the order but already charged the card
    *   The order was lost in your warehouse because of misplaced paperwork
3. The customer claims unauthorized use of a credit card. This could be due to any of the following:
    *   Lost credit card or identity theft
    *   Friendly fraud (misuse of card by a family member)
4. Merchandise was returned but refund has not been issued. This could be due to any of the following:
    *   Your accounting department dropped the ball (that's why it is important to have a business process).

- The customer didn't notice that the credit had already been issued to the statement, less the shipping charges.
5. The customer cannot reach you to dispute the charge. Some companies make it difficult for customers to contact them, so it's easier for the customer to dispute the charges and let the merchant jump through the hoops.

Chapter 21.

When Hell Freezes Over: Analyzing Data

You will go to Ecom Hell if: *you do not pay attention to your business data.*

If you put off becoming a marketing expert on your business until hell freezes over, if hell ever freezes over, chances are you will be there to see it happen.

Note: See "Promoting Your Store" for a discussion on the roles and responsibilities of the marketing department.

Web Analytics

When Google purchased Urchin software in 2005, they leveled the playing field for small-business owners competing with larger retail rivals. By making the tools available for the right price (*free*), they have helped owners understand where their store traffic is coming from, which keywords are converting, and which marketing campaigns are returning positive ROI. Google's goal is to get small businesses to advertise more on AdWords by providing the tools to understand store metrics and help give customers a better user experience.

After I started using Google Analytics in 2006, I became a much better marketer, and our business really took off. I am by no means an expert; I still consider myself a student, as there is always something new to learn about web analytics. But what I can tell you is that this is worth your time if you are focusing on the right data.

There are tons of books out there on web analytics. One of my favorites is *Web Analytics: An Hour a Day* by Avinash Kaushik. I do not geek out on the data; I just focus on the metrics that I know I can positively affect. There is only so much time in a day, so I looked at a few key metrics and did not worry about the rest. I am sure I left some money on the table by not scrutinizing every little detail, but in the grand scheme of things, we were meeting our goals and I was pleased with our revenue growth.

How much time you want to spend on analytics is completely up to you, especially if you are wearing many different hats in your company. Learning about analytics is well worth your time, even if you are hiring someone to help you manage marketing.

One of the metrics I look at is bounce rate, or the percentage of visitors leaving a site without clicking onto another page (that is, they click the back button or enter another URL). This metric tells you how sticky your website is to your visitor. Less sticky sites have higher bounce rates; the stickier a site is, the longer a visitor stays.

If you are working on social media, pay attention to direct-traffic data, comparing before-and-after Twitter or Facebook campaign results, to see how effective your brand is in the social space. This is one way to determine the ROI of your social media strategy.

If you are going with a Yahoo! Store, be sure to sign up with Monitus. net to capture your sales transactions for Google Analytics.

Here are some other metrics that you can use to track and measure the success of your business. Consistently review all of these metrics. Create a spreadsheet or Access database to help manage these data. Do comparisons month by month and year by year. Look for variances in the report. Ask yourself why there are variances and whether you need to take action on them. Note and annotate exceptions and all activities in Google Analytics.

(Google Analytics is coming out with a Universal Analytics[3] that will allow you to add your offline metrics to your Google Analytics tools. Check it out to see if it will help you manage your data.)

Web Metrics Tips

- Review bounce rate by URL (landing pages).
- Review bounce rate by top content.
- Review the landing page with the lowest bounce rate and compare it with higher bounce rate pages to identify the differences.
- Segment your report by traffic source: specific referrer, paid search, organic search, etc.
- Know the ecommerce visit value for your primary keywords.
- Study traffic referrers, and compare data with prior years, if available, noting how results are affected by marketing campaigns and SEO efforts.
- Review top exit pages. What can you do to stop the exodus of visitors?
- Review your sales funnel (funnel conversion rate). Make sure goals are set up properly. For example, if ten thousand added to your cart but only nine hundred actually checked out, this is a less than 1 percent conversion rate. You need to understand where/why visitors are dropping off so you can reduce your shopping cart abandonment rate. A decent funnel conversion rate is somewhere between 20 and 35 percent (sales confirmation).
- Compare categories over prior years to see what has changed. For example, if you added new items to a category, you should see an uptick in page views and higher average price per period, as well as product revenue and transaction increases.
- Compare unique visitors monthly for this year and last year.
- How long where visitors on your site? Measure time on site.
- How many of your visitors came back? Look at your return visitor data.
- Check the bounce rate and conversion rate for your top 10 to 20 money keywords.

---

3 http://support.google.com/analytics/bin/answer.py?hl=en&answer=2790010.

- Determine the number of page views per visitor.
- Determine shopping cart abandonment, and set shopping cart funnel goals.
- Pay attention to your average order value and figure out ways to increase this amount to generate higher top line sales.
- How many were visitors? How many were qualified visitors? How many actual buyers?
- How many came in looking for your brand?
- Average per visit value?

Useful Social Metrics

- Number of Fans on Facebook
- Number of followers on Twitter
- Number of re-tweets for your tweets
- Number of people in your Google + circles
- Number of comments on your blogs, Facebook,
- Number of shares for your video's by your fans
- Number of times photos are viewed or shared
- Number of likes on your facepages and on your actual sites
- Number of user engaged in conversation with your company.

Useful Financial Metrics

- Demand sales (daily, monthly, and annual comparison)
- Gross sales
- Net sales (after cost of goods sold)
- Gross margins
- Gross margins by product category (compare on a monthly basis)
- Shipping and handling revenue (as a percentage of total sales)
- Net income
- Budget comparison (track quarterly)
- Daily bank deposits and weekly cash flow report
- Free shipping cost versus sales revenue with and without free shipping

Useful Merchandise and Inventory Metrics

- Sort by category (men, women, kids, flowers, gifts, apparel, furniture, etc)
- Daily, monthly, quarterly revenue (compare year over year)
- Sales percentage by category
- Back orders for inventory from vendors
- On-hand inventory value, clearance value, and obsolescence value
- Inventory turnover
- Days of inventory (how much you have on hand and what you can ship)
- Product margins (in-house inventory, drop-ship items, profits by category)

Useful Operations Metrics

- Number of calls taken by CSR, calls in the queue, cost per contact, average waiting time
- Number of calls by types (orders placed, returns, refunds, order status follow-up)
- Number of packages shipped per day, month, and year
- Number of products produced per day, month, year
- Pending orders (on back order, due to inventory, not in stock)
- Customer satisfaction through customer surveys
- Number of orders processed per day, per hour
- Number of emails responded to each day

The most important aspect of your metrics is to be consistently measuring and sharing them across your organization. Using one set of dashboards or spreadsheet will help ensure that your team members understand the marketing and operational goals.

Testing Site and Landing Pages

Testing in the context of ecommerce means you are comparing different website design elements against a set control group. Your goal is to determine if any of the minor or major tweaks you make helps you reach your goals faster. In this case, the goal is to increase sales by dollar amount, whether it's upping the average dollar per color or the conversion rate. Use Google Analytics to track the number of visitors coming to your website and then the number who become actual paying customers who place real orders.

There are two kinds of tests. First, there is the A/B test, which compares one control group to another control group. The second is called multivariate testing, which means one control group with one set of elements is tested against the same control group with different elements, and all the different variations and combinations in between, to realize the maximum conversion rate for your website.

With A/B testing, you might test the "Add to Cart" button against a button with different wording, such as "Buy Now." With multivariate testing, however, you might test the position of the "Add to Cart" button on the page as well as whether it works better with multiple product images, hero shots, or keywords and whether one font or style is better than another. Multivariate testing has lots of moving parts and can get complicated, which is why it's useful to use specialty testing software to benchmark your progress.

Landing pages are the most frequently tested pages. Although you could probably argue that all the pages on your website are landing pages, the conversion community refers to a landing page as the page to which you intend to take your visitor. For example, when you run a PPC campaign, you take visitors to a specific landing page that you have ideally already run tests on for high conversion outcomes. Or when you send out email campaigns, you take them to a promotional landing page that is proven to produce the maximum sales per email run.

The truth is, however, that most ecommerce storeowners, large or small, do not run landing page tests consistently. Landing page testing is not a one-time project. This is an ongoing, never-ending (you hope) task that keeps you excited about what you do as a marketer, because you are constantly moving the needle upward and increasing sales and conversion rates.

Look into Google Website Optimizer and Optimizely.com

Increasing Conversions

Storeowners frequently discuss increasing conversion rates. One thing that I have learned is that the bigger brands or big-box retailers like Office Depot will have higher conversion rates than smaller stores. However, if your niche is very targeted, you can enjoy a pretty good conversion rate as well, though you may wonder how that is possible. My own opinion (based on data that I have seen) is that big brands usually enjoy conversion rates of above 12 percent and higher. Most smaller ecommerce stores hover around 0.09 to 1.5 percent, and more targeted niche sites might hover around 1.75 to 3.5 percent. Experts agree that if you're seeing around 1.5 to 3.5 percent, you're doing pretty well, though there is always room for improvement.

Big brands have better conversion rates because they spend a lot of money advertising their brand, they usually have a brick-and-mortar presence, and they have name recognition. Customers have already built some trust in the organization, and as a result, when those customers add products to their cart, it's either because they need them (office supplies) or they feel comfortable that their order will be shipped and any problems will be taken care of.

This is why smaller stores need to work harder to make visitors feel comfortable and inspire confidence. They need to go the extra mile to make their websites look professional and to make it easy for visitors to navigate.

Tips for Increasing Conversion Rates

- Have product reviews or customer testimonials.
- Offer a free-shipping program.
- Display shipping costs on product pages, not just on the shopping cart.
- Have a professional-looking, easy-to-navigate website.
- Offer an excellent internal search tool.
- Use professional product photos.
- Offer targeted promotions with expiration dates.
- Include coupons and discounts.
- Provide social widgets for gaining traction (like Facebook's "like" button).

- Ensure good product content written using correct spelling and grammar.
- Study internal site search data for merchandising tips and product suggestions.

Internal Site Search Tool

One goal in designing an online store is to make your site user-friendly. In addition to having useful menus and uncomplicated navigation features, an internal site search will help your visitors explore your site more easily. Unless you are selling only a couple of items and your website has only a few pages, your search box can help your site provide a better user experience.

Have you ever visited a site and left exasperated because you could not find what you wanted? Frustrating, isn't it? Don't let your visitors go through this. With internal site search, you can provide easy site navigation, especially to first-time visitors. This will help them get around your site and quickly find what they are looking for. It is especially useful if you are regularly adding new items and content.

The more easily your customers can find what they want, the more satisfied they will be, which elevates the possibility of conversion. Visitors want to find products and service information as quickly as possible. They do not want to waste time clicking through menus. If your visitors cannot find what they are looking for right away, don't be surprised if they leave and go directly to your better-organized competitor.

With the right search tool, your site search data (that is, the words and phrases visitors enter into your site's search box) can provide valuable insight into your customers' behavior. More effective than customer feedback gathered from focus groups or surveys, as well as less intrusive, the internal site search provides information on who visits your site and how they find their way around, revealing which pages they visited, which searches prompted them to stay longer, and which searches made them leave the site. This collected data is helpful when analyzing conversion rate performance for each section of your site.

Once implemented, internal site search can collect lots of keywords for you. It is a great source for determining popular search terms and helping you collect keyword terms that you may have not thought of. In addition, by continually reviewing your site search data, you can tweak your site's content according to user demand. Keep in mind, however, that optimizing for internal search is different from optimizing for external search; people search for generic terms in search engines, whereas they look for specific items in your site. So be sure to continue with your SEO efforts, while also paying extra attention to keywords that visitors use once they arrive in your site.

Tapping your internal site search for ideas is a great way to generate fresh content, promote popular items, or offer new products. Whatever your visitors search for in your site is what they expect to see, read about, or purchase. If you notice a huge number of visitors searching your site for a certain type of product or service, you should consider addressing that demand, even if it is not currently part of your offering. Since your site is already driving traffic for those searches, you might as well turn it to your advantage.

An optimized internal site search can reduce bounce rate, as satisfied visitors stay longer, thus increasing the chances of quality conversion. Make sure to place the site search box in a conspicuous location on your site. I have used SLI Systems, a third-party solutions provider, as well as Nextopia. com, for our Yahoo! stores.

Consider the following tips when reviewing your internal site search for new keywords and material.

Customer Insight

What keywords have led visitors to your site? What are they looking for? Analyze your site search logs or use Google Analytics to learn your visitors' search behavior. Know what they are looking for, how often they search, and what they do next. Your data will serve as your benchmark as you improve your site's search function.

Relevancy

Improve the odds of having people find what they're looking for within the first pages of the search results. You can do this by optimizing your site's content and product titles, as well as by leveraging the keywords most often searched and the popular items visitors click on.

Refining Searches

Showing too many results can frustrate visitors. Allow site users to narrow down results by enabling filtering tools. Common criteria are brand, product, age, size, style, and color. Look into faceted search or navigation, it's a technique that allows users to filter criterias base on what they are looking for. Zappos.com does a really good job with this feature.

Sorting

Instead of narrowing down results, allow visitors to use the "sort by" tool to get prioritized query results. This enables them to sort according to product price, user rating, and date of product arrival, for example.

Misspellings

Visitors may sometimes misspell words in your site search box. Naturally, these would return "0 results found." Avoid these negative results by identifying common misspellings in your site search logs and adjusting your search tool's vocabulary accordingly. Or you could use any paid intelligent search tools like Bazaar Voice, which suggests commonly searched terms as you type.

Customer Reviews

One of the main reasons a customer fails to buy is fear that the product will not live up to its potential or that they'll have buyer's remorse. More than ever, customers are looking for value and reliability. An effective way to close a sale is to assure customers of their purchase beforehand and help them make purchasing decisions by offering product reviews.

Third-party solutions, like PowerReviews.com (now Bazaar Express), make it easy to bring product reviews into your product pages. Alternatively, use your ecommerce platform's integrated product review feature and invite customers to review your products. To be credible, reviews should include both praise and criticism. (Amazon.com features "the best review" alongside "the most useful review," even if it is critical.)

Giving customers a forum on which to share stories and offer testimonials is a great way to incorporate social media and lend third-party credibility to your product pages. Include social bookmarking icons, such as Facebook and Pinterest, so that customers can share with their networks when they "like" a product.

Whenever possible, include unique product videos and how-to advice, tips, and tricks. Begin with your best-selling products, higher-conversion products, and products exclusive to your store. It may sound like a lot of work to produce and post these items, but they really do shore up purchasing decisions and ultimately, they make your site more useful to customers.

Chapter 22.

Growing Your Business

You will endure in Ecom Hell if: *you do not know what your end goal is.*

Business, more than any other occupation, is a continual dealing with the future; it is a continual calculation, an instinctive exercise in foresight.

—Henry R. Luce

I am a big believer in beginning with the end in mind. In other words, know your outcome. What is your purpose? Is this business your retirement fund? Are you starting this business because you lost your job? Are you bored and just looking for something to do? Sure, it's fun creating a business; it's something new and exciting to look forward to. However, the hardest part is the daily grind. You may hear about overnight success stories in the media, but this rarely happens in the real world. If and when success does happen, the journey usually takes years of hard work and it only seems like an overnight success to others.

Knowing your exact purpose and goal—whether to sell your business, retire, or flip it and start something else—will help keep you motivated and on track during the fight to the finish.

"Without continual growth and progress, such words as improvement, achievement, and success have no meaning."

—Benjamin Franklin

Now that you have set up your business, growing it is one of the most exciting aspects of owning your own business. This is where you get to be a little more creative in devising and implementing marketing plans. The key to successfully growing your business is to manage expectations (*yours, your customers', and your employees'*) and to be consistent. Make sure you stick to the plan, even in the weeks that the marketing campaign did not do so well. The key is not to abandon the plan but to figure out why things did not work and why they were working before and then tweak accordingly.

One lesson I have learned is not to grow too quickly, especially if the infrastructure is not in place to handle the growth. In addition to my own experiences, I have seen other companies, including those of my vendors, go through similar growing pains. Constantly putting out little fires can make your life truly miserable. Managing your expenses and cash flow is essential to the successful growth of your company. Invest capital in areas of your business that will return revenue for you. For example, when managed wisely, advertising will have a much better ROI for your company than a new souped-up monitor or piece of office furniture.

Fine-tuning your company to operate around a customer's needs (i.e., being customer-centric) is one way to be competitive online, where the goods are mere commodities and where only the truly customer-driven organizations will thrive and grow. How you sell and interact with customers is often just as important as what you sell. As your company grows, reinvest in such areas as website usability, enhancing user experience, better navigation, better product merchandising, and better content written with the customer's needs in mind.

Your job is to engender consumer confidence in your brand. One way to achieve this is to have credibility within your customer reviews. Publish both the good and the bad reviews to give customers a true picture of a specific product or service. If you want to make money and have a successful business, focus on and take care of your customers and your employees.

Your job is to ensure that your company's value proposition is clear and that customers and employees know exactly what value you bring to the table.

As much as you might like to think that you can do everything yourself, knowing which areas require hired help is critical. Look for people who will help grow your business and delegate. As your company grows, do not continue to hire people who all report to you. Instead, create a hierarchy of staff to share your responsibilities so you can focus on the overall business.

As the owner/CEO of your company, another of your primary responsibilities is recruiting. Always be on the lookout for people who can help you grow your company or contribute to your company by adding a skill set that you do not have or that is far superior to yours. It's always good to hire and have people on your team who are smarter than you.

This is also a crucial time to focus on being the leader of your company. Commit your time to listening to your people—really hearing their concerns and their inputs on how to grow and improve your company's process. Work on a plan to create an organization development that organizes how your company functions. Review and audit your business processes, fine-tune your knowledge base, and champion areas that need improvement by allocating proper resources to making the experience better, not just for your customers but also for your employees. Subscribe to the belief that happy employees equal happy customers; this philosophy will help you focus on meeting the needs of your employees, especially as your company experiences growth. The key to success is to experience that growth without the pain.

As your company grows, you may incur more expenses related to new employees—more computers, more employee benefits, increased salaries, and perhaps even a move to bigger offices or warehouses (my company moved four times in four years between 2004 and 2008). You must really watch your budget at all times. Money in the bank can camouflage your growing expenses. As you add more fixed costs to your operations, you will also need to work harder to increase sales at a comparable, or preferably higher, rate than before.

Stay ahead of your industry, and pay attention to your competition. Above all, work on being the leader in your category. The idea is to have the competition watching and copying you, instead of the other way around.

Develop business partners and strategic alliances that will help move your business ahead. Always know where your revenue is coming from a year in advance, but be nimble enough to see changes in market trends. Be prepared to take advantage of opportunities that make sense for your business.

However, be guarded about distractions. Cleverly disguised as opportunities, distractions will come knocking on your door in many forms, usually at a time when you feel like you can conquer the world. You've gotten this far because you were focused; now is not the time to dilute your efforts with another project with "potential." Ignore the shiny penny.

Reflecting back on my own experiences, as well as countless stories from friends, family, and clients, a key factor for success is having a cohesive strategy for each aspect of your business. Having a cohesive strategy means that whatever you decide to do, it is synergistic with your objectives and how you plan to get there. For an ecommerce business, every level and aspect of your company, from the website, systems, and processes to employees and customers, should all come from this strategy, so that customers have a consistently high-quality experience.

As your company grows, refine and review your business processes to ensure that they still apply. Make modifications where necessary. Controlled growth makes forecasting easier when major shifts in operations and processes need to happen. Assess whether roles and responsibilities are changing and growing with your company and goals. Consider that in a growing company, wearing too many hats can burn employees out very quickly. Is it time to recruit talent to help your struggling staff?

Once you have mastered your business process and operations, you can start thinking about developing new websites. My company had seven different websites from 2004 to 2009. We were able to leverage our infrastructure (e.g., customer service, accounting, warehousing, and marketing) to help us grow our revenue. Most ecommerce businesses have more than one website. For example, Wayfair.com consolidated more than two hundred niche ecommerce stores into one brand. This made sense for them as they specialized in home consumer goods, a rather broad category.

I would be remiss if I did not mention that you should also have a plan for downturns. Sometimes, the economy is not the cause for a downturn in business; sometimes, there is too much competition in the marketplace or changes in search engine algorithms that negatively affect online traffic to your website. Whatever the case, you need to have a plan B ready just in case. By being prepared, you will be proactive, rather than reactive, in implementing solutions. Look for opportunities during downturns or slow sale cycles; take this time to retrain employees and regroup with your team to formulate new strategies to gauge market opportunities.

As much as any entrepreneur would love to experience unbridled growth, the best strategy for sustainability is to achieve controlled growth.

Do not try to be everything to everybody. Only after you perfect your core competencies can you move into other growth models. Watch your expenses during this growth period. There is a tendency for companies to burn through cash reserves at a rate that does not align with their revenue growth.

One of the reasons why companies go through growing pains is that the information within each department are confined within their internal departments. The left hand and right hand are not connected and people within the organization are not aware on what is going on else where in the company. One way again to solve this is to share data via spreadsheets or online dashboards.

Gearing Up for Busy Seasons

Most ecommerce entrepreneurs greet the holiday season with both sheer joy and utter dread. While you relish the influx of orders, you also dread the long hours, untold stress, and the hard work that comes with actually earning the customer's business. The key to surviving and thriving for the holiday season is extreme preparation.

Consider the rest of the year as a dry run, a test, if you will. If you have created a successful marketing plan, you will see your efforts really pay off during the holiday season. Customers will buy almost anything during the holidays, if the product is presented correctly. Therefore, it's imperative that you take the opportunity to prepare your staff, your operations, and your vendors for the busy season. Your business process must be nailed down. There will be no time to learn on the fly. Anything short of being prepared—whether it's having enough inventory on hand or having enough employees to process and ship the goods—will not only result in missed sales opportunities but could also hurt your brand and future revenue.

The holiday season is not the time to roll out major changes on your website or try the new back-end software. All this must be done and completed before September, so that you have enough time to fix and find solutions to your process before the busy season actually hits. Normally, the traffic quadruples right around Black Friday (the day after Thanksgiving), with some retailers experiencing an increase in traffic as early as October. So be prepared! The bottom line is there is no such thing as being overly prepared for the holiday season.

Chapter 23.

Hidden Sources of Revenue (Bonus Section)

Since the bulk of the book is focused on the basics of getting your ebusiness up and running, I wanted to leave you with a few more advanced strategies and marketing tips that can help generate additional income from areas you may not have thought of yet. The next section explores some hidden sources of revenue you may want to tackle after mastering the basics.

Personalization and Customization

Embroidering and engraving are value-added services that you can sell as add-ons to products. This can be either outsourced to a third party or done in-house, so long as you realize there will be some capital investment in equipment rental and labor. Does offering customization make sense to you? If you sell items that are frequently monogrammed, such as towels and silver pieces, it may be a natural way to increase margins. Research the cost of providing the service, minus the upcharge to customers, to determine how quickly you'll be able to recoup the investment.

Your competition may not offer these extra services, so adding them could be part of your unique value proposition.

Gift Cards and Gift Certificates

As more people embrace the idea of giving gift cards and gift certificates, you will want to consider this value-added service as another way to promote your business. By offering gift cards, you provide a one-size-fits-all gift option to shoppers, especially those who are unsure of what to buy. Gift cards and gift certificates can also encourage brand loyalty among customers, as well as gain new customers, especially during the holidays. Take advantage of the demand for online gift cards and gift certificates to boost sales and to market your brand to new customers.

Today, gift certificate providers, such as GiftTango.com, can help you provide virtual gift certificates through email and mobile forms. Some, like Cashstar.com, even offer features for customization and either online or in-store redemption. Once you have the program in place, don't just sit there and expect to ring up gift card sales. Maximize your gift card and gift certificate program by treating it just like a product that you want to sell. Announce the availability of gift cards and gift certificates in a conspicuous place on your website. List your gift cards by category on your home page and navigation bar. Mention online gift cards and gift certificates in your newsletters, in a dedicated email (e.g., for last-minute holiday shoppers), in print advertisements and flyers, and in any other advertising medium you use.

Motivate customers to purchase gift cards and gift certificates online by offering a bonus gift card (e.g., an extra ten dollars with the purchase of a one-hundred-dollar gift card). You might also try saving an abandoned shopping cart with an email follow-up suggesting a gift card. You'll know if the items in the cart were intended to be gifts if your shopping cart function allows a gift check box ("This item is a gift"). This will enable you to segment and only send emails to those abandoning gift items.

Loyalty Programs

A customer loyalty program is a marketing strategy designed to incentivize return clientele and to reward regular customers for their loyalty. In general, incentives come in the form of special offers, discounts, points, or rebates. As the name suggests, a loyalty program is about nurturing and fostering relationships with customers. This should not be undertaken simply because you desire overnight results. That's not to say that you might not get immediate results from this type of program, just be sure to set expectations realistically, over the long term. Developing a well-thought-out loyalty program requires some patience. While your program may start out as a simple rewards system, in the long run, there's more to loyalty programs than just dangling a carrot in front of customers. A successful program must have communication with the customer that flows two ways; that is, customers gain benefits while you learn about them and their preferences.

To ensure the highest level of participation, keep your program simple. Complicated rules will annoy even the most loyal customers. How do customers become members? Do they need to purchase a certain amount to qualify? How are points redeemed? Do they need to sign up online? Be sure to test every step in the process to identify and resolve issues before launching. You do not get a second chance to make a first impression, and getting customers to return after a bad first experience is very difficult.

In addition to tangible rewards, offer soft benefits that build emotional connections. Soft benefits, like exclusive previews of new products or specially arranged express delivery, can enhance your brand's value proposition. Although material rewards can move most people, personal attention and convenience encourage greater commitment. Further enhance a loyalty program by finding the right partners who can add flexibility and additional benefits for customers. Ensure that the partnership is in alignment with your objectives and that it can make your program more effective.

Loyalty programs also allow customer segmentation and profiling. Evaluate your customers and categorize them according to their value to your business. Profile purchasing behavior, demographics, and lifestyles. Use the data to identify trends, analyze how customers react to a particular promotion, and increase conversion.

Remember, the long-term goal of loyalty programs is customer retention. A program's success lies in your ability to use the information you gain to segment, tailor campaigns appropriately, and build upon the excellent customer satisfaction you foster by customizing rewards to the customer's preference.

More Bonus Material

Ecommerce Success Tips

Ecommerce is getting more and more competitive every day. The big-name brands are pouring huge resources into their websites. Here are some tips on how you can compete:

- Stay nimble and flexible. Companies that can adapt, spot trends, and take action quickly can have huge advantages. For example, as a small-business operator, you can take advantage of opportunities for an "inventory buy" at discount prices. Likewise, you can easily pivot when your email campaign message is not working.
- Adopt new technology. If you have the budget, don't be afraid to invest in new technology that can save you time and labor and give you better data. When used properly, these tools can help you take strategic action and see huge gains. Apps are a great way to get new technology at an affordable monthly cost.
- Build your email list as soon as you can.
- Build your mobile commerce as soon as you can, especially if you're selling directly to the consumer.
- Get involved in social media right away. Start connecting with your customers as soon as possible. They will not only become loyal customers, but they will also send new customers your way.
- Always be looking for new products that your customers would want to buy. You have to stay on top of the hottest, the latest, and the greatest of what your customer base is looking for. They are going to spend their money somewhere; the only question is where.
- Be consistent. This is the hardest for small-business owners. There can be so much distraction. If you don't set up your business correctly right from the beginning, you will be managing by fire or will constantly be in crisis mode—even if you are experiencing successful sales. You need to work on your business work process

flow and be consistent in following your company procedure. If you follow your procedures, your employees will likely do the same. Remember, it's easier to train for good habits than to break bad ones.

- Always strive to learn. Attend industry webinars (most of them are free) and go to trade shows and conferences.

- Focus on your core strength and outsource or hire for your weakness. If you focus on increasing skill levels instead of working on things that you do not like or that do not come naturally, you will have a higher ROI and will be better able to leverage your strength. For example, if you do not like working with numbers, hire a bookkeeper; just make sure you are still actively looking at the reports and taking action on them.

- Get rid of slow-moving items. This is especially important if your industry is fashion focused. The general rule of thumb is that inventory more than seven months old is usually marked down 50 to 75 percent. If you're in the fast-fashion industry, you change out every six weeks. This will allow you to turn over your slow sellers, clear up warehouse space to bring in new products, and replenish your cash flow. Be sure to learn why the merchandise didn't sell, as this will help you avoid future buying mistakes and help you promote what does sell on your website. Remember, inventory is cash, and "Cash is king."

- Do what your competition does not or offer what they are unwilling to offer.

Taking Care of Yourself

Starting a business is both emotionally invigorating and exhausting. Most entrepreneurs burn the candle on both ends. But of course this is a big mistake. You need to take care of yourself by eating well and exercising. Owning your own business is highly stressful. If you are not taking care of yourself, you're not going to be around to enjoy your success when it finally arrives. To most people, this is called being burned out.

By taking care of yourself, you can enjoy the daily journey. Your daily experience can be enriching and rewarding as you learn new skills, meet new people, and discover yourself a little more in the process.

Here are some tips to help you enjoy the journey:

- Always strive to learn. I cannot say this enough. The journey is just as much about personal growth as it is business growth.
- Help others. Contributing to others will help you live a more fulfilling life.
- Be grateful. Count your blessings. Yes, the to-do list and the list of problems are a mile long. But you "get to" work on them because you own your own business. How cool is that?
- Don't beat yourself up when you make mistakes. Everyone makes mistakes. You will make more mistakes than you will hit home runs. Just make sure that your home runs are the big ones that count.
- Pat yourself on the back. Recognize your efforts and hard work.
- Trust your gut instinct. Listen to the little voice in your head—it's usually right.
- Be flexible. The most flexible and adaptable person wins. It's a dynamic world, and change is inevitable.
- Eat well and exercise regularly, even if it's just walking for thirty minutes a day.
- Get lots of sleep. Being tired all the time will make you cranky, which, in turn, will make you no fun to be around.
- Schedule everything, even family time—in fact, especially family time. One of my favorite Anthony Robbins quotes is, "What's talked about is a dream. What's envisioned is exciting. What's planned becomes possible. What's scheduled is real."
- Multitasking is the enemy of focus. Many entrepreneurs are proud of and even brag about their multitasking abilities. But what I've learned over the years is that it's difficult to do several things well, much less actually accomplish and complete multiple tasks in a timely manner. Focus on only a few tasks (the magic number is three) and get them done. Don't add more to the list until one is completely checked off.

- Do not let being a perfectionist make you procrastinate. Too many entrepreneurs get bogged down in being a perfectionist. But putting off rolling something out because everything is not perfect can be just an excuse. Be aware of the true reason for the delay. Sometimes, good enough is good enough. Roll out your business, website, campaign, or product, and continue working toward perfection.

Your Homework:

1. Decide how you are going to prepare your website and your staff for the busy season.
2. Develop a promotional campaign that would strengthen the loyalty of your customers.
3. Think of additional services which you can offer to customers. This must be something that is not offered by other businesses as a way to differentiate your brand.

Chapter 24.

Selling Your Business

There may come a time when you choose to sell your business. Perhaps the occurrence will be something that you have to do out of necessity, or maybe it was your goal right from the start. Perhaps you like to start businesses but are not too keen on maintaining them. It takes different types of people and personalities to do either or both.

Selling my business was one of the hardest decisions I had ever made. In 2008, I realized that to take my business to the next level, I would have to invest a lot more money. Since I was not willing to bet the family farm, I decided to sell. But before that could happen, I knew my business processes had to be standardized and systematized. Most of the pieces were already in place, but they needed fine-tuning. So we focused on that in preparation for the sale.

I found my own potential buyers by making a list of who's who in the industry and determining who would be a good potential buyer. Eventually, I connected with my buyer. After nine long months of due diligence, we reached an agreement.

You can always show potential buyers your growth in revenues, but if your business model does not lend itself to being profitable, then it will be hard to find a buyer. You will only get paid for what your business is currently making times a multiple (usually somewhere between three to six times, depending on the industry). Therefore, you must grow top line revenue as well as net income.

You also need to make sure that your knowledge base is up-to-date and accurate. This valuable selling point is an asset that you have built. This knowledge base is your company's intellectual property, and it will help your business become a turnkey opportunity for the buyer.

Review Chapter 4 for the list of tips on buying a business. The future owner/buyer will want to know answers to the questions on the list. The key to a successful sell is being able to justify the asking price. The new owners will be thinking about how long it will take to get a return on their investment—Two years? Three years? Or more? The buyer will compare to see which businesses will be a better investment and likely provide a better return at a lower risk.

Different types of buyers will be looking for different metrics. There are owner/operator buyers, and there are investors. Both types of buyers will be focused on top-line revenue (gross sales). Smaller business buyers are looking at capital investment, purchase price, and annual income. Bigger buyers will also consider how the acquisition will add percentage of growth to their existing top-line revenue. They will want to know if they can absorb your current operations into their own and how they can leverage their existing economies of scale. Your final net income is another big factor in calculating your selling price. Obviously, the more you make, the higher price you can ask, as you have a proven business model that is already profitable. Be extra careful on what you share in terms of information if your potential buyer is a competitor. You want to be forth coming but you also to agree to show in deeper details about the business once a letter of intent is signed.

Don't agree to an earn-out, which is something you would want as a buyer of a business but as a seller, you lose control of the business and once the new owner take over, it's difficult to really ascertain if changes in revenue is due to any changes made after the sale or the business didn't live up to its potential. Speaking of money, try to get all your money up front or within a relatively short period, even if you take a little less, cash is King and you'll have peace of mind knowing that your financial future is secure.

Ideally, you want multiple offers/bids before you settle on accepting the buyer's letter of intent. There are many different ways to structure a sale. It is important to seek the advice of an attorney and consult with your accountant/CPA to come up with a value to your business based on revenue and income. You may also decide to consult a business broker; if so, be sure to ask for a list of references of similar size and type (ecommerce) businesses that have been listed and sold before. Having attorneys help with the transaction is going to be very helpful but at the same time, don't let the attorney's battle of egos blow up the deal. Keep them focus on moving forward to closing the deal.

Don't get caught up in what you think your business potential might be. Most businesses are not sold on potential (at least, most buyers are not willing to pay for that). Instead, focus on making your business easy to take over, able to be operated as a truly turnkey business. Just like most home-buyers like to move in to a brand-new/newly remodeled home, business buyers like to walk into their new office and start depositing the profits into the bank.

If I had only one piece of advice to share about selling your business, it would be to know why you want to sell. Do you want to retire early? Is there a family crisis/emergency forcing a change? Are you not making enough money? Know the real reason why you are selling so that you don't regret doing this later.

Finally, once you have sold your business, give yourself permission to enjoy the end game. Don't jump right into another venture (like I did). Your mind and body need to rest. If your finances permit, take some time off to restore and renew your energy levels so you can be at the top of your game when the next opportunity arises.

A Parting Thought

I will be forever grateful to all the friends, colleagues and clients that have allowed me to share and learn from them. Starting and running a business is not easy, but it can be one of the most rewarding experiences of your life. I hope you will not expect perfection in all the things that you learn from this book but to aim for progress instead as in life, business is work-in-progress. Be sure to celebrate success along the way and reflect on lessons learned from the mistakes that you made.

And that folks, is a wrap. I hope you enjoyed reading this book as much as I did writing it.

I would love to hear from you. You can reach me at shirleytan@ecommercesystems.com if you have any questions, need clarification, or if you want to hire me.

I would appreciate your feedback on the book at Amazon.com, good and bad...hopefully good. Thank you very much for honoring me with your valuable time, and I hope that we get to connect real soon. I usually attend the Internet Retail Conference; I hope to see you there.

Appendix

Resources, References, and Tools

Affiliate Programs

- Commission Junction
- LinkConnector
- LinkShare
- ShareASale

Analytics

- Google Analytics
- Monitus.net
- Yahoo! Analytics
- Clicktale
- Crazyegg

Back End

- Stone Edge Order Manager
- QuickBooks Enterprise (This is now better at managing inventory.)

Must-Read Books

- *Web Analytics 2.0*, Avinash Kaushik
- *Pinterest Marketing*, Jennifer Evans Cario
- *Landing Page Optimization 2*, Tim Ash
- *The Art of SEO*, Eric Enge and Stephen Spencer
- *YouTube and Video Marketing,* Greg Jarboe
- Emyth book series, Michael E. Gerber
- *Advance Web Metrics*, Brian Clifton

Comparison Shopping Sites

- PriceGrabber
- Shopping.com
- Nextag

Email Marketing Tools and Others

- Aweber
- Constant Contact
- Mailchimp
- Bronto
- Top Right for Yahoo! Stores
- Vertical Response
- SiteTuners.com—Attention Wizard Tool
- Infusionsoft

Gift Card and Certificate Programs

- GiftTango.com

Keyword Research Tools

- Market Samurai
- Wordtracker.com
- Google AdWords

Search Engine Optimization Tools

- Moz.com
- MajesticSeo.com—Backlink Tool
- Spyfu.com
- Raventools.com
- SeoToolSet.com—BruceClay.com

Merchant Accounts

- Emerchant.com, Bill Dumont
- Faircommerce.com, Bob Bryant

Other Payment Processors

- Google Wallet: This tool ensures that your customers will be able to check out quickly and securely when shopping on your site.
- PayPal: Offers people the opportunity to pay for their merchandise without divulging personal information to strangers. It has been estimated that PayPal processes 24 percent of US online payments.

Accounting and Order Processing

- Roxanne Brown—Quickbooks Expert, rox@consulting4qb.com
- SalesTax.com
- Quickbooks

My Favorite Google Tools

- Google Alert
- Google Webmaster Tools
- Google Merchant Center
- Google Drive
- Google AdWords
- Google Gmail
- Google Insights
- Google Trends

Yahoo! Store Designers

- YourStoreWizards.com
- ExclusiveConcepts.com
- EYStudios.com
- PracticalData.com
- Fastpivot.com
- KingWebmaster.com
- Ytimes.com

Outsourcing

- Guru.com
- Odesk.com
- Elance.com
- Fiverr.com

Cloud-Based Tools

- Basecamp.com: Collaboration tool
- Podio.com: Collaboration tool
- Dropbox.com: Cloud-based storage
- Evernote.com: Note-taking tool
- ZenDesk.com

Ecommerce Platforms

- Yahoo! Small Business
- Magento
- Volusion
- Groove Commerce
- Big Commerce – go to ecommsystems.bigcommerce.com and your trial period will get extended out.

Internal Search Tools

- Bazaar Voice
- Nextopia – enter "ECOMBOOK" in checkout to get 10% off all packages
- SLI Systems

Other Useful Tools and Sites

- Ispionage.com—Competitive Analysis
- Optimizely.com—A/B Testing Software
- Live Chat by Liveperson.com
- Freemindmap.com—Mind-mapping tool
- TurntoNetworks.com—Social Commerce
- MarketMotive.com—Online Training

- Trust-Guard.com — www.trust-guard.com/ecom-hell-book-offer - to get your special pricing and 60 day free trial from Trust Guard.

Glossary

404 error page. An HTTP (hypertext transfer protocol) response when a user requests a page not available on the website. This happens when the link is wrong or not available on the website anymore. This error message indicates that although the web browser could establish connection with the server, what was requested could not be found.

above the fold. The upper half of the front page of any newspaper. This space often captures the most important news or photograph. Since the papers are folded in half and the upper half is displayed to customers, this is the most viewed part of the newspaper. For this reason, this space is also the most preferred for advertisers as well. The same is true for websites. The higher the ad appears on the page, the better the chances of people viewing it.

affiliate. A website that is linked to a main website (known as a merchant website) and routes traffic to main websites. The affiliate and merchant are bound through an agreement, which consists of a number of people who are referred from affiliate to merchant site.

alias (inventory). In inventory management, alias (or item code) refers to the creation of different names given to products from vendors and customers. Thus, it provides an ability to sell items under different aliases even though they were bought under a different item code / alias from the vendor.

alt text. For SEO—for images—alt text, as the name says, is an alternative text representation for any image. This might be useful when the browser does not show any graphics. Hence, the user will not lose out on any information on the website.

anchor text. The visible or clickable part of a hyperlink. It is usually in blue and underlined and takes the user to the relevant link. Use of correct keywords in the anchor text will ensure a rank for the page. If numerous websites link to a site for a particular anchor text keyword, the search engine will likely attribute anchor text to be relevant and an authority for that site.

autopopulate/ suggest. Search tool—this tool automatically populates data by giving suggestions before the user finishes typing completely. This helps users save time as well as gives keyword suggestions for the search.

AVS number. Address verification system number through which the merchant establishes the ownership of the credit/debit card. This system essentially checks the address and ZIP code of the card user and compares it with the address associated with the credit card company. This system verifies only numerics of the address and therefore might lead to false declines if the addresses are input in a different manner.

back end. Also referred to as the back office, back-end technology in ecommerce is used to process online orders, inventory management, accounting integration, etc.

backlink. Incoming links that are pointed to a website. Presence of more links means the website is popular and is relevant to the search engines.

barrier to entry. Hurdles that prevent new companies' easy entry into the market. The reasons can include technology, regulations, heavy setup costs, fierce competition, strong customer loyalty, etc. Strong barriers to entry protect the existing companies and help retain their market share.

blind shipping. A shipment that does not reveal the point of origin. This is used by many ecommerce retailers of late. In simple words, the person receiving the package will not know where it has been shipped from. The business would not want the customer to see the name of the original supplier to protect the source.

bounce rate. Refers to the visitors who drop from viewing additional web pages on the website. In these cases, the visitor only views the first page and then leaves the site.

breakeven point. A point where businesses make neither profit nor loss. At this point, the revenue earned equals the costs incurred. Graphically, it is the point where the total cost curve and total revenue curve meet.

brick-and-mortar. A conventional retailer that operates out of a building is termed as brick-and-mortar. These companies interact with customers face-to-face.

business-to-business (B2B) channel. All transactions between two businesses with respect to information, products, or services rather than individuals. The latter is termed as B2C or business-to-consumer, whereby the end client is the consumer or general public.

canonical URL. The one authoritatively correct URL for a website. When a website can be accessed via multiple URLs, a canonical URL should be identified. All alias URLs for a resource should redirect to the canonical URL to enforce its authority. For example, www.yourdomain.com/index is the same as www.yourdomain.com and this may cause duplicate-content issues when the index page is actually the same as the main website page or home page.

cash flow. Money moving in or out of a business. Cash flow always has a period of time and is usually a result of investing, operations, or financing. Cash flow is used to calculate various metrics of a business like rate of return, liquidity, and capital to operate the business, etc.

chargeback. The reversing of a credit card transaction on the request of the cardholder instigated by the credit card companies. Chargebacks might happen because of merchant errors at the point of sale or because of fraudulent transactions, etc.

click-through rate (CTR). The count of clicks that happen on an advertisement in proportion to the number of times the advertisement is played. This measures the effectiveness and success of an online advertisement campaign. A high click-through rate implies relevancy of advertisements to the user.

comparison-shopping engine. Also known as CSEs, comparison-shopping engines compare specific products on multiples ecommerce websites. They help the user choose a product based on price, attributes, etc. Comparison-shopping engines do not sell the products; however, they earn commissions when the user clicks on the link in the search results.

content network. A large distributed system of servers deployed in multiple data centers on the Internet to serve high content availability and performance to end-users.

conversion. The percentage of visitors to a website converting into customers for a sale, sign up, or any call to action that is set as a goal.

conversion optimization. Also called a conversion-rate optimization (CRO), conversion optimization is a technique of creating an effective landing page for a visitor focusing on converting the visitors into customers.

converting keyword. This is a keyword that is highly recognizable by the visitors to a website and enhances the chances of conversion.

cookie. A small amount of data from a website that is saved in the user's web browser. Cookies track the user's browsing history and movement on the website and store them in a file. This helps in resuming browsing exactly where it is paused or in remembering information that the user has provided, such as login IDs, passwords, email addresses, etc.

costs of goods sold (COGS). The costs associated with production of goods and/or actual cost of goods. This includes material and labor costs. Costs related to distribution, sales, and administration, which are termed *indirect costs*, are not a part of COGS. Revenue minus cost of goods sold reflects gross margin or cost of sales.

cost-per-click. Also known as pay-per-click, an online advertising concept through which website owners drive traffic to their respective websites. In this model, the advertisers pay the website owners based on the number of clicks on their website. In some cases, when the required number of clicks is achieved, the advertisements are removed from the website. In simple terms, cost-per-click is the amount incurred to ensure a click on the advertisement.

coupon code. A special discount offered on a purchase made in an online or ecommerce environment. Coupon codes consist of alphabets or numbers or both. In order for customers to use the code, they enter the code while checking out of an ecommerce website. Coupon codes motivate the buyers to shop with a particular seller online because of the benefits they receive. The benefits could be in the form of discounts on purchase of products, a freebie on purchase, cash-back offers, waiver of shipping costs, etc.

cross-channel selling. Reaching out to customers through various distribution channels. Through this, we use one channel to drive sales into another channel. For instance, online advertisement may lead to increased foot traffic in a physical store. While this concept has gained popularity recently, in the past, channel conflict was treated as a concern because of the fear of losing market position. Online, cross-channel generally refers to selling on Amazon Marketplace, eBay, and other comparison-shopping sites as well as one's own ecommerce website.

cross sell. The practice of selling or proposing alternative/additional products or services to the customer. This method of selling is very effective in increasing sales. An instance of cross selling is to suggest selling a bedsheet set when a blanket has been added to a shopping cart.

countdown tool. Small codes embedded in the main code of a website, which helps in introducing a countdown timer (e.g., days to go for birthday), on the website.

CSS (website design coding). A sheet styling language used to describe the look and format of a document; commonly, web page applications are written in HTML or markup language(language HTML, XML, etc) from the presentation aspects (color, layout, font, etc).

customer relationship management (CRM). This is a business system, usually a software, that manages all touch points of customer (current and prospective) interaction with an organization. This could include but is not limited to sales and marketing, after-sales service, technical support, etc. This helps with better understanding of the customer, customer retention, acquiring new customers, increased profits, reduced costs, etc.

customer service representative (CSR). The point of contact for an organization to interact with its customers. CSRs help resolve customer queries or troubleshoot their problems. They are usually termed as "the face of the company," as they are the people with whom the customer interacts, in regards to questions or concerns. Some organizations use them to enhance sales, while some use them only to solve customer queries.

CVV number. Also known as card verification value, it is a three- or four-digit number on the reverse side of credit or debit cards. While on Visa, MasterCard, and Discover, it is a three-digit number, on an American Express card, it is a four-digit number. CVV numbers are also known as CSC (card security code) numbers or CVV2 numbers. When the cardholder provides a CVV number to an online merchant during a transaction, it establishes that the user actually has the debit or credit card physically and thus reduces fraud.

DBA (doing business as). A legal term used in the United States of America to represent the name under which the business operates if it is different from the registered name.

dedicated hosting. Means a client/customer does not share the server with anyone else and has access to the entire server. This is not a shared hosting where the resources are divided between multiple clients. The advantage of dedicated hosting is having complete control of the servers, as well as being able to use an operating system or any hardware of the user's choice.

doorway page. Also known as an entry page, jump page, or bridge page, refers to a web page designed with the objective of achieving a better placement in search engine rankings and driving traffic to their website. This is achieved by inserting the keywords, in the form of hidden text, which the search engine picks up. Search engines frown upon and usually penalize websites using doorway pages.

drip campaign. An automated series of emails (multistep) sent over a period of time to prospective customers. Each step is referred to as a drip. Drip campaigns are very low maintenance, which is one of the reasons they are so successful. This term comes from a phrase used in agriculture, *drip irrigation*, which refers to watering plants in small doses over a period of time.

drop ship. An online selling technique in which the retailer doesn't keep stock of products and instead passes on customer orders and other details like shipping addresses directly to the wholesaler and in some cases, the manufacturer. The manufacturer/wholesaler then dispatches the products to the customer directly. In this model, the retail price minus the wholesale price is the profit of the retailer.

DSS compliant. Also termed as "payment card industry data security standard (PCI DSS)," this refers to the data security standard in the card industry. In order to ensure there are no security lapses while using debit or credit cards online, organizations need to adhere to certain security standards designed by credit card organizations like Visa and MasterCard.

dynamic keyword insertion (DKI). An advance feature of Google AdWords is one that dynamically updates the text to include the keywords used or those that match a customer's query. DKI helps target specific and relevant customers, and the bolded text ensures the advertisement is recognized instantaneously thus increasing the click-through rate.

earn-out. A variable part of the price paid to acquire a company. When the business meets the targeted revenue, the seller would be entitled to extra pay based on the achieved revenue.

ecommerce. Electronic commerce is the business carried out in the online retail space where the web acts as a common platform bringing the buyers and sellers together.

email campaign. A message sent to a number of people using email. This includes sending emails to existing customers for the purpose of retention as well as sending emails to prospective customers. Email campaigns are also used to create brand awareness. Email marketing has an advantage of reaching out to a large number of people compared to other mediums. It is also cheaper, measurable, and targets a specific audience.

email opt-in. When customers agree to and sign up to receive emails. On the other hand, emails sent without customers' consent are termed as spam. Opt-in emails are usually promotional in nature and relevant to the user's needs or interests and can be in the form of a newsletter or can simply be information about products.

employee ID number (EIN). Applicable to the United States of America, also known as federal tax identification number, it is issued to business entities. This is free and provided by Internal Revenue Service (IRS).

evergreen category. For online businesses, this means categories or niches that always have customer demand and have existence that is more of a necessity than a luxury. This evergreen niche strategy helps the websites to attract visitors on a long-term basis.

GEO targeting tool. When a website wants to target customers in a specific geography, Google offers customized results for the query. Hence, the results returned to a query of a user in California are different from the results returned in New York. This concept of geographically customizing the search results would not impact the appearance of a website in search results.

Google AdWords. An advertising product that has the highest revenue generator for Google, the company. Through Google AdWords, a business can advertise its product by displaying ads to users who have searched for it on Google or other affiliated sites. Google AdWords works on a pay-per-click model and serves local, national, and international users.

HTML. Stands for hypertext markup language and is a programming language used for designing web pages for Internet browsing. It consists of plain texts as well as HTML tags.

iFrame. An architecture that prevents search engines from seeing what content is residing inside the iFrame; iFrames are not recommended if SEO is important on a website for search engines to be able to index its content. The purpose of an iframe (internal frame) is not to prevent search engines from seeing what is going on; the purpose is to include information from another url into the current page. For example, a positive use of an iframe is to include a YouTube video into a sales page.

inbound links. Links that connect to your website. Inbound links are also referred to as black links. A higher number of inbound links indicates the popularity of the website; the website is considered more relevant in searches than similar web pages.

ISP. Stands for Internet service provider, also known as internet access provider (IAP). ISP is an organization that offers Internet access. There are various types of Internet service providers like DSL, fiber-optic service, wireless, and dial-up with varying levels of service, which the user should consider before selecting a service provider. Connection speed and price are the two most important factors users consider before selecting an Internet service provider.

Javascript. One of the programming languages that is popular across the world. Javascript is an HTML language for web, PCs, tabs, laptops, and many more. It is a programming code and can be inserted into an HTML page.

key performance indicator (KPI). A performance measurement system that evaluates an organization's growth toward its goals and objectives. Key performance indicators (KPIs), also known as key success indicators (KSI), are quantifiable and consensual to determine success measures for any organization. These vary from organization to organization and are aimed to achieve operational and strategic targets.

keyword density. Refers to the number of times the keyword appears on a web page. It is the percentage of times the keyword is located on the web page among all other content. This determines the relevancy of the website to a keyword. Too much keyword density risks overoptimization and can get your site banned by search engines.

landing page testing. The test captures the click sequences for visitors to a website and utilizes the post-click data analysis to identify pages that produce the best return on investment.

legacy system. An obsolete computer system, technology, or program. This might also refer to processes or terminology no longer in use or still in use but no longer supported by its original maker.

link farm. A group of websites all linked to each other. This is created only to increase the popularity of links, thereby gaining a better ranking. A link farm's content consists mainly of hyperlinks and is usually random and not related to other websites. Search engines frown upon link farms and are aggressively going after sites that are involved in link farms.

link value. Measures the worth of a link. The most popular method of computing a link value is based on the quantity and quality of the site that is giving the link. The higher the quality and number of quality links, the better it is.

load time. The time taken for a web page to load or reload, substantially or completely. It is the time taken for the browser to load the page completely from the time the server receives the request.

long-tail keyword. Longer yet more specific keywords, usually as long as five words. Long-tail keywords are more specific and, therefore, draw highly relevant traffic to the website and likely increase the chance for conversion.

manufacturer's suggested retail price (MSRP). The price that the manufacturer of a product suggests to be sold in market is the manufacturer's suggested retail price. The retailers may or may not use the MSRP, and the customers may not want to pay the MSRP. Sometimes, retailers reduce the prices to much less than MSRP for low-demand products.

margin. Refers to the differential of a cost price and selling price of a service or product. It is usually referred to as a percentage of product marked up from cost that results in the gross profit on the markup.

margin markup. Refers to the percentage of the cost price, which is added to get the selling price.

merchant account. The payments on ecommerce platforms are enabled through the setup of merchant accounts, which help businesses to accept payments made through credit or debit cards.

meta description. An HTML attribute that gives precise descriptions of the contents on a website. Search engines use these on results pages to show snippets of a page.

minimum advertised price (MAP). An agreed price between retailers and suppliers, wherein the retailer specifies the least possible price that it is allowed to be sold at. If the retailer violates the agreement, suppliers may choose to no longer do business with the retailer.

mobile commerce. The concept of buying and selling products or services from mobile devices.

mobile-optimized version. Making a website easily viewable from a mobile phone. This is important as the number of cell phone users is greater than the number of Internet users and there is a steady increase in the number of smart phone users, which make mobile commerce easier.

monthly account fee. The monthly fee paid for managing the account on a website.

multichannel capabilities. Refers to the presence of a business on multiple channels for a customer (e.g., eBay, Amazon, Magento, Shopping.com, Walmart Marketplace, etc).

negative keyword (Google AdWords). These are the keywords that keep the advertisements restricted to the intended visitor and not to visitors who are looking for something else. For example, if you're a wedding photographer, a negative keyword for your ad might be "wedding" because it's too broad.

net profit. The profit made by an entity after deducting all the costs incurred. Net profit is also referred to as bottom line, net earnings, or net income. Net profit is arrived at after deducting the overhead costs and interest costs.

niche market. Refers to marketing efforts targeted at a specific, relevant, and small population. The target segment is identified by analyzing their needs and creating goods or services to address the same. This is also known as micromarketing.

"No follow" (SEO). A value/tag assigned to an HTML element that desires that search engines should not be influenced by the presence of a hyperlink on a web page while calculating the website's ranking. It's basically telling the search engine to ignore the tag area that is "not followed."

Occupational Health and Safety Administration (OSHA). The US agency that ensures the public is protected from safety hazards. They also offer consultation services, such as telephone support, on-site visits, partnerships, etc, with the objective of reducing occupational hazards and illness.

off-page optimization. Optimization of factors that affect the ranking of a web page in the search engines. These factors are out of the website owner's control as it appears on other websites (e.g., page rank and link popularity).

one-way links. When a site links to yours, but your site does not link back to theirs. One-way links are one of the ways to increase link popularity resulting in the increase of the site ranking. This sends out a strong message to the search engines that your website is extremely valuable and that other people would like to know about it.

on-page optimization. Refers to factors that impact the listing of the web page on the search engines. These are controllable through coding of the page, e.g., keyword placement, meta tags, on-site interlinks, website architecture, etc.

open graph. A type of protocol developed to enhance the visitor experience and provide the provision of one common login for many interfaces so that multiple functionalities are availed by just one ID.

organic search results. Search results based primarily on the relevance of content and not influenced by any advertising. These are the websites that appear on Google, for example, below the sponsor section, which is usually about three paid sponsors for any given keywords.

pay-per-click (PPC). An advertising tool that directs traffic to websites. The visitors are directed to a particular website when an ad is clicked. PPC is also known as cost-per-click.

payment gateway. A service that authorizes online credit and debit card transactions by facilitating communication between the card user, the business, and the bank. The payment gateway decreases the amount of time spent processing payments and provides fraud protection.

PCI (payment card industry) compliance. A set of data security standards that are designed to provide the most comprehensive single framework to address all the security, integrity, and privacy of the data of customers.

persistent shopping cart. This is a code developed in the website that helps the website to remember the preferences of a customer even when he or she has left the page. The information is saved until the customer's next visit.

pop-up. An Internet marketing tool, pop-ups capture the visitor's attention and lead him/her to different websites, different parts of a website, or a call to action or capture the email addresses or other contact information for a database.

promotion header. Heading tags and content that are placed above the sidebars with the purpose of enticing a visitor to click links that may lead to a sale of products or services.

product feed. A master document that is the repository of all the information about the services and/or products of a company on the ecommerce platform. These are usually in the form of .csv or .xml to allow a bulk upload of inventory data to another platform. For example, if you want to sell on Google Shopping, you would provide an updated (sometimes daily or hourly) product feed so that your products will appear as part of Google Shopping search.

proprietary code. Codes that are not openly available and regarded as trade secrets by developers.

quality score. The keywords, ads, and landing pages need to be judged on the basis of their relevance to the visitor. This rating is calculated by Google; there is no official explanation of how the quality score is determined. The going consensus, however, is that the higher the quality scores the less the ad may cost the advertiser and perhaps aid in the placement of the ad on the search results page.

reciprocal link. A mutual link between two websites where the visitor from website A is led to website B and vice versa thus enhancing mutual visibility. These types of links may cancel each other out in terms of link value, but they still provide some value to the site visitors.

return on investment (ROI). A financial measure of performance. ROI is calculated as the return on investment divided by the total cost of investment made.

return-to-vendor (RTV) items. Items that have crossed their aging standards or are damaged and can be accepted by the vendors as returned products. The terms and conditions for returns are governed by vendor and customer agreements.

RMA (return material authorization) form. Used to return the goods/products to a vendor / supplier as agreed upon according to the company policies. RMA numbers are also issued to the customer, because it helps a company keep track of what is being returned back to their warehouse.

robot.txt files. A text (not HTML) file that is put on the website to advise the search robots which pages should not be visited. It is not a protection or prevents search engines from crawling the website.

RSS (rich site summary) feed. Provides a full or summarized text, plus metadata such as publishing dates and authorship of the blogs, news entries, audio, video, headlines, etc. RSS feeds syndicate the content automatically and keep the reader up-to-date.

sales funnel (Google Analytics). Refers to any set of actions that lead a visitor on a website to a desired completed action. This may or may not result in actual sales. Sales funnel analysis provides insights to businesses to increase effectiveness of the websites in capturing customers and achieving goals.

search engine optimization (SEO). A technique to increase the visibility of a website on the search engine. The probability of a viewer visiting a site is improved if the site is ranked in the search results as a top-five rank or on the first page.

SEO ranking. SEO analysts try to analyze a website structure that includes but is not limited to common terms searched by users and actual terms in search engine results and, as a result, accordingly tries to modify the content of a website. Effective SEO strategy can help a website to achieve a higher rank in search engine results.

session ID. Refers to a uniquely identifiable number that a website's server assigns to a specific visitor for the duration of that user's visit (session). It can be stored in different forms (i.e., cookie, form field, or URL).

shared hosting. Also called virtual hosting, refers to a web-hosting service where many websites utilize the space of a web server that is connected to the Internet. Each website is allocated separate partitions in order to separate from other sites.

site bread crumbs. Navigation tools that provide a trail for the website visitor to follow back to the starting or entry point. Bread crumbs usually appear horizontally across the top of a web page and provide links back to each previous page the user navigated through to get to the current page.

site-wide link. Links that are present on every page of a site and are usually placed in the footer or sidebar of a site.

social bookmarking. According to Wikipedia, this is a way for Internet users to organized, edit, store, and share bookmarks of web documents. Examples of social bookmarking sites are Digg, Reddit, and Delicious.

social network. Refers to a network of individuals/organizations and similar entities that interact through web-based technologies and the dynamics of network relations between them.

spam. The use of electronic messages to contact a large customer base through sending unsolicited bulk messages. The most common form of spam is email spam. It can also refer to links from undesirable websites or sites that offer no value to users—commonly referred to as spam blogs (splogs)—to websites that are trying to game the search engines.

spam laws. CAN-SPAM act of 2003, (Controlling the Assault of Non-Solicited Pornography and Marketing). The law does not specifically address non-optin emails, only the ability for someone to opt-out. Thus an email marketer may still get emails from partner's email lists.

split test. Also known as A/B testing, it is an approach to compare and contrast two different designs of a website. A test is in the form of a contest between two versions of images or buttons that are being optimized to increase the website conversion.

SSL (Secure Socket Layer) certification. Protocol uses a third party, a certificate authority (CA), to identify one or both ends of the transactions, thus ensuring secure transactions between web servers and browsers. An organization / business needs to install SSL Certificate(s) onto its web server for secure sessions with browsers.

static page. A standard web page using only HTML (hypertext markup language) that doesn't involve employing dynamic technologies like PHP, ASP, Perl, etc. Static pages result in standard URLs displaying the same information for all users and are usually more search engine friendly.

sticky. The content published on a website that is put up with the objective of getting a user to stay on a site or return to a website. Such content helps in engaging the attention of the viewer and may make him/her spend more time on the site.

SWOT analysis. A strategic business analysis metric involving understanding of strengths, weaknesses, opportunities, and threats for a business. Strengths and weaknesses are internal to the business while opportunities and threats are external.

terminal ID (TID). A unique number that is linked to a specific point-of-sale (POS) terminal and is used to identify the merchant operating the terminal during debit/credit card sales transactions. TID numbers are used to set up online processing through payment gateways.

text file transfer. A technique to transfer files over the Internet. It involves converting the code page of a file from one code page to another page. It also involves converting CRLF (carriage return-line feed) characters between different systems.

tiered discount. Discounts that are offered on different tiers/bundles, e.g.:

Buy $500+ of items from A, get a 3 percent discount

Buy $1000+ of items from A, get a 7 percent discount

Buy $2000+ of items from A, get a 10 percent discount

title tag. Defines the title of a document. These are essential for all HTML/ XHTML types of docs. A title tag tells the search engine about the web page; thus, it becomes an essential part of the SEO strategy of a website.

trust seal. A sign of security and trustworthiness of the website. It is grant-ed usually to the entire website or for businesses for display. It typically signifies presence of reliable security practices / methods for transac-tions through the website.

turnkey solution. A form of a readymade system that can be easily imple-mented into current business processes. A turnkey solution is imme-diately ready to use upon implementation and is designed to fulfill certain processes depending on the industry.

uniform resource locator (URL). A pointer to resources on the Internet. A resource can refer to a file/directory/query/database/search engine, etc. In common parlance, a URL is known as a web address. YourDomain. com is your URL.

unique value proposition (UVP). A powerful message that reflects the uniqueness of a product or service of a company / business. It is usually a differentiator from competition in the marketplace.

up sell. A sales method in which a seller tries to convince a customer to purchase additional products or upgrades in order to increase the total sale amount.

up-time (hosting account). The quantum of time for which a server has stayed up and running. It is generally referred to in percentage, like "98.89 percent up-time." It is one of the metrics used to analyze the performance of a web-hosting provider.

XML (extensible markup language) feed. These feeds are a way of paid inclusion where a search engine is provided information about an ad-vertiser's web pages by XML. Spider-based search indexes use the XML feed that represents the advertiser's website. Usually, marketers have to pay to get these services. This is also used extensively by drop shippers as a way to get orders from their customers into the drop shipper's back-end.

XML (extensible markup language) sitemap. XML (extensible markup language) sitemap - an XML file containing a list of web pages and URLs. Webmasters can submit the file manually or wait for the search engines to crawl on the links.

watermark (for images). An image or pattern in which a business/organization can be recognized. It usually appears as multiple shades when seen in direct or reflected light. The variations in thickness, density, material, and translucency of the medium also affect the watermark. The watermark is used for easy identification as well as copyright purposes.

Index

17065279R00147

Made in the USA
San Bernardino, CA
29 November 2014